The Search For Meaning Series
Viewpoints in American History

I

A Nation Established

Richard E. Marshall

John Edward Wiltz

J. B. LIPPINCOTT COMPANY

Philadelphia • New York

The Lippincott Social Studies Program

Supervised by

STANLEY E. DIMOND

School of Education
University of Michigan

Dr. Dimond has served as Divisional Director, Department of Social Studies, Detroit Public Schools, and is Professor of Education in the School of Education, University of Michigan. In addition to supervising the Lippincott Social Studies Program, Dr. Dimond is the author of *Schools and the Development of Good Citizens,* and co-author of *Our American Government* and *Civics for Citizens.*

About the editors

Dr. Marshall is Professor of History and Political Science, Montgomery County Community College, Blue Bell, Pennsylvania. He has been a teacher and department chairman in social studies at the secondary level. He received the M.S. degree in the teaching of social studies in secondary education, M.A. in international relations, and Ph.D. in international relations. He has been a lecturer at Pennsylvania State University and Chestnut Hill College.

Dr. Wiltz is Associate Professor of History at Indiana University. He has been a visiting lecturer at the University of the West Indies in Jamaica and a guest professor of history at Hamburg University, Germany. He is the author of *In Search of Peace: The Senate Munitions Inquiry, 1934–36; From Isolation to War: 1931–41; Books in American History: A Basic List for High Schools;* and *The Search for Identity: Modern American History.* He is co-author of *The Teaching of American History in High School.* Dr. Wiltz was for five years associate director of the Lilly Program in American History, a project dedicated to improvement of the teaching of American history in the secondary schools of Indiana.

Cover design by PMD Services

Printed in the United States of America

4.732.1

ISBN-0-397-40207-4

The documents and reading selections in the Search for Meaning series have been chosen to represent the differing and frequently conflicting points of view that have marked the course of American history. In *A Nation Established* the people of the period describe their times, the major events, and issues in the story of America from early Viking settlements through the period before the Civil War.

CONTENTS

DISCOVERY AND SETTLEMENT

Voyages of the Northmen to Vinland

The *Saga of Eric the Red* is a narrative which tells of the voyages of the Northmen (Vikings) to Vinland (the continent of North America). It is difficult to determine exactly when this narrative was composed, but most scholars believe it to have been written down between 1200 and 1300 in Iceland. The following excerpt from the *Saga* describes Vinland, the inhabitants, trading, and the Northmen's decision to return home.*

... They sailed for a long time, and until they came at last to a river, which flowed down from the land into a lake, and so into the sea. There were great bars at the mouth of the river, so that it could only be entered at the height of the flood-tide. Karlsefni and his men sailed into the mouth of the river, and called it there Hop [a small land-locked bay]. They found self-sown wheat-fields on the land there, wherever there were hollows, and wherever there was hilly ground, there were vines. Every brook there was full of fish. They dug pits, on the shore where the tide rose highest, and when the tide fell, there were halibut in the pits. There were great numbers of wild animals of all kinds in the woods. They remained there half a month, and enjoyed themselves, and kept no watch. They had their live-stock with them. Now one morning early, when they looked about them, they saw a great number of skin-canoes, and staves were brandished from the boats, with a noise like flails, and they were revolved in the same direction in which the sun moves. Then said Karlsefni: "What may this betoken?" Snorri, Thorbrand's son, answers him: "It may be, that this is a signal of peace, wherefore let us take a white shield and display it." And thus they did. Thereupon the strangers rowed toward them, and went upon the land, marvelling at those whom they saw before them. They were swarthy men, and ill-looking, and the hair of their heads was ugly. They had great eyes, and were broad of cheek. They tarried there for a time looking curiously at the people they saw before them, and then rowed away, and to the southward around the point.

Karlsefni and his followers had built their huts above the lake, some of their dwellings being near the lake, and others farther away. Now they remained there that winter. No snow came there, and all of their live-stock lived by grazing. And when spring opened, they discovered, early one morning, a great

number of skin-canoes, rowing from the south past the cape, so numerous, that it looked as if coals had been scattered broadcast out before the bay; and on every boat staves were waved. Thereupon Karlsefni and his people displayed their shields, and when they came together, they began to barter with each other. Especially did the strangers wish to buy red cloth, for which they offered in exchange peltries and quite gray skins. They also desired to buy swords and spears, but Karlsefni and Snorri forbade this. In exchange for perfect unsullied skins, the Skrellings would take red stuff a span in length, which they would bind around their heads. So their trade went on for a time, until Karlsefni and his people began to grow short of cloth, when they divided it into such narrow pieces, that it was not more than a finger's breadth wide, but the Skrellings still continued to give just as much for this as before, or more.

It so happened, that a bull, which belonged to Karlsefni and his people, ran out from the woods, bellowing loudly. This so terrified the Skrellings, that they sped out to their canoes, and then rowed away to the southward along the coast. For three entire weeks nothing more was seen of them. At the end of this time, however, a great multitude of Skrelling boats was discovered approaching from the south, as if a stream were pouring down, and all of their staves were waved in a direction contrary to the course of the sun, and the Skrellings were all uttering loud cries. Thereupon Karlsefni and his men took red shields and displayed them. The Skrellings sprang from their boats, and they met then, and fought together. There was a fierce shower of missiles, for the Skrellings had war-slings. Karlsefni and Snorri observed, that the Skrellings raised up on a pole a great ball-shaped body, almost the size of a sheep's belly, and nearly black in color, and this they hurled from the pole up on the land above Karlsefni's followers, and it made a frightful noise, where it fell. Whereat a great fear seized upon Karlsefni, and all his men, so that they could think of nought but flight, and of making their escape up along the river bank, for it seemed to them, that the troop of the Skrellings was rushing towards them from every side, and they did not pause, until they came to certain jutting crags, where they offered a stout resistance. Freydis came out, and seeing that Karlsefni and his men were fleeing, she cried: "Why do ye flee from these wretches, such worthy men as ye, when, meseems, ye might slaughter them like cattle. Had I but a weapon, methinks, I would fight better than any one of you!" They gave no heed to her words. Freydis sought to join them, but lagged behind, for she was not hale; she followed them, however, into the forest, while

Saga of Eric the Red in J. F. Jameson (ed.), ORIGINAL NARRATIVES OF EARLY AMERICAN HISTORY, Vol. I, Charles Scribner's Sons, 1906.

the Skrellings pursued her; she found a dead man in front of her; this was Thorbrand, Snorri's son, his skull cleft by a flat stone; his naked sword lay beside him; she took it up, and prepared to defend herself with it. The Skrellings then approached her, whereupon she stripped down her shift, and slapped her breast with the naked sword. At this the Skrellings were terrified and ran down to their boats, and rowed away. Karlsefni and his companions, however, joined her and praised her valor. Two of Karlsefni's men had fallen, and a great number of the Skrellings. Karlsefni's party had been overpowered by dint of superior numbers. They now returned to their dwellings, and bound up their wounds, and weighed carefully what throng of men that could have been, which had seemed to descend upon them from the land; it now seemed to them, that there could have been but the one party, that which came from the boats, and that the other troop must have been an ocular delusion. The Skrellings, moreover, found a dead man, and an axe lay beside him. One of their number picked up the axe, and struck at a tree with it, and one after another [they tested it], and it seemed to them to be a treasure, and to cut well; then one of their number seized it, and hewed at a stone with it, so that the axe broke, whereat they concluded that it could be of no use since it would not withstand stone, and they cast it away.

It now seemed clear to Karlsefni and his people, that although the country thereabouts was attractive, their life would be one of constant dread and turmoil by reason of the [hostility of the] inhabitants of the country, so they forthwith prepared to leave, and determined to return to their own country. . . .

Discovery of America

The entire daily journal of Columbus' first voyage to America covers the 225-day period from August 3, 1492 to March 15, 1493. The segment reprinted here includes the period from October 10 through October 14, 1492.*

WEDNESDAY, 10TH OF OCTOBER

The course was W.S.W., and they went at the rate of 10 miles an hour, occasionally 12 miles, and sometimes 7. During the day and night they made 59

*Journal of the First Voyage of Columbus in J. F. Jameson (ed.), ORIGINAL NARRATIVES OF EARLY AMERICAN HISTORY, Vol. I, Charles Scribner's Sons, 1906.

leagues, counted as no more than 44. Here the people could endure no longer. They complained of the length of the voyage. But the Admiral cheered them up in the best way he could, giving them good hopes of the advantages they might gain from it. He added that, however much they might complain, he had to go to the Indies, and that he would go on until he found them, with the help of our Lord.

THURSDAY, 11TH OF OCTOBER

The course was W.S.W., and there was more sea than there had been during the whole of the voyage. They saw sandpipers, and a green reed near the ship. Those of the caravel Pinta saw a cane and a pole, and they took up another small pole which appeared to have been worked with iron; also another bit of cane, a land-plant, and a small board. The crew of the caravel Niña also saw signs of land, and a small branch covered with berries. Every one breathed afresh and rejoiced at these signs. The run until sunset was 27 leagues.

After sunset the Admiral returned to his original west course, and they went along at the rate of 12 miles an hour. Up to two hours after midnight they had gone 90 miles, equal to 22½ leagues. As the caravel Pinta was a better sailer, and went ahead of the Admiral, she found the land, and made the signals ordered by the Admiral. The land was first seen by a sailor named Rodrigo de Triana. But the Admiral, at ten o'clock, being on the castle of the poop, saw a light, though it was so uncertain that he could not affirm it was land. He called Pero Gutierrez, a gentleman of the King's bed-chamber, and said that there seemed to be a light, and that he should look at it. He did so, and saw it. The Admiral said the same to Rodrigo Sanchez of Segovia, whom the King and Queen had sent with the fleet as inspector, but he could see nothing, because he was not in a place whence anything could be seen. After the Admiral had spoken he saw the light once or twice, and it was like a wax candle rising and falling. It seemed to few to be an indication of land; but the Admiral made certain that land was close. When they said the Salve, which all the sailors were accustomed to sing in their way, the Admiral asked and admonished the men to keep a good look-out on the forecastle, and to watch well for land; and to him who should first cry out that he saw land, he would give a silk doublet, besides the other rewards promised by the Sovereigns, which were 10,000 maravedis to him who should first see it. At two hours after midnight the land was sighted at a distance of two leagues. They shortened sail, and lay by under the mainsail without the bonnets.

FRIDAY, 12TH OF OCTOBER

The vessels were hove to, waiting for daylight; and on Friday they arrived at a small island of the Lucayos, called, in the language of the Indians, Guanahani. Presently they saw naked people. The Admiral went on shore in the armed boat, and Martin Alonso Pinzon, and Vicente Yañez, his brother, who was captain of the *Niña*. The Admiral took the royal standard, and the captains went with two banners of the green cross, which the Admiral took in all the ships as a sign, with an F and a Y and a crown over each letter, one on one side of the cross and the other on the other. Having landed, they saw trees very green, and much water, and fruits of diverse kinds. The Admiral called to the two captains, and to the others who leaped on shore, and to Rodrigo Escovedo, secretary of the whole fleet, and to Rodrigo Sanchez of Segovia, and said that they should bear faithful testimony that he, in presence of all, had taken, as he now took, possession of the said island for the King and for the Queen his Lords, making the declarations that are required, as is now largely set forth in the testimonies which were then made in writing.

Presently many inhabitants of the island assembled. What follows is in the actual words of the Admiral in his book of the first navigation and discovery of the Indies. "I," he says, "that we might form great friendship, for I knew that they were a people who could be more easily freed and converted to our holy faith by love than by force, gave to some of them red caps, and glass beads to put round their necks, and many other things of little value, which gave them great pleasure, and made them so much our friends that it was a marvel to see. They afterwards came to the ship's boats where we were, swimming and bringing us parrots, cotton threads in skeins, darts, and many other things; and we exchanged them for other things that we gave them, such as glass beads and small bells. In fine, they took all, and gave what they had with good will. It appeared to me to be a race of people very poor in everything. They go as naked as when their mothers bore them, and so do the women, although I did not see more than one young girl. All I saw were youths, none more than thirty years of age. They are very well made, with very handsome bodies, and very good countenances. Their hair is short and coarse, almost like the hairs of a horse's tail. They wear the hairs brought down to the eyebrows, except for a few locks behind, which they wear long and never cut. They paint themselves black, and they are the color of the Canarians, neither black nor white. Some paint themselves white, others red, and others of what color they find. Some paint their faces, others the whole body, some only round the eyes, others only on the nose. They neither carry nor know anything of arms, for I showed them swords, and they took them by the blade and cut themselves through ignorance. They have no iron, their darts being wands without iron, some of them having a fish's tooth at the end, and others being pointed in various ways. They are all of fair stature and size, with good faces, and well made. I saw some with marks of wounds on their bodies, and I made signs to ask what it was, and they gave me to understand that people from other adjacent islands came with the intention of seizing them, and that they defended themselves. I believed, and still believe, that they come here from the mainland to take them prisoners. They should be good servants and intelligent, for I observed that they quickly took in what was said to them, and I believe that they would easily be made Christians, as it appeared to me that they had no religion. I, our Lord being pleased, will take hence, at the time of my departure, six natives for your Highnesses, that they may learn to speak. I saw no beast of any kind except parrots, on this island." The above is in the words of the Admiral.

SATURDAY, 13TH OF OCTOBER

"As soon as dawn broke many of these people came to the beach, all youths, as I have said, and all of good stature, a very handsome people. Their hair is not curly, but loose and coarse, like horse hair. In all the forehead is broad, more so than in any other people I have hitherto seen. Their eyes are very beautiful and not small, and themselves far from black, but the color of the Canarians. Nor should anything else be expected, as this island is in a line east and west from the island of Hierro in the Canaries. Their legs are very straight, all in one line, and no belly, but very well formed. They came to the ship in small canoes, made out of the trunk of a tree like a long boat, and all of one piece, and wonderfully worked, considering the country. They are large, some of them holding 40 to 45 men, others smaller, and some only large enough to hold one man. They are propelled with a paddle like a baker's shovel, and go at a marvellous rate. If the canoe capsizes, they all promptly begin to swim, and to bale it out with calabashes that they take with them. They brought skeins of cotton thread, parrots, darts, and other small things which it would be tedious to recount, and they give all in exchange for anything that may be given to them. I was attentive, and took trouble to ascertain if there was gold. I saw that some of them had a small piece fastened in a hole they have in the nose, and by signs I was able to make out that to the south, or going from the island to the south, there was a king who had great cups full, and who possessed a great quantity. I tried to get them to go there, but afterwards I saw that they had no inclination. I resolved to wait until to-morrow in the afternoon and then to depart, shaping a course to the S.W., for, according to what many of them told me, there was land to the S., to the S.W., and N.W., and that the natives from the N.W. often came to attack them, and went on to the S.W. in search of gold and precious stones.

"This island is rather large and very flat, with bright green trees, much water, and a very large lake in the centre, without any mountain, and the whole land so green that it is a pleasure to look on it. The people are very docile, and for the longing to possess our things, and not having anything to give in return, they take what they can get, and presently swim away. Still, they give away all they have got, for whatever may be given to them, down to broken bits of crockery and glass. I saw one give 16 skeins of cotton for three *ceotis* of Portugal, equal to one *blanca* of Spain, the skeins being as much as an *arroba* of cotton thread. I shall keep it, and shall allow no one to take it, preserving it all for your Highnesses, for it may be obtained in abundance. It is grown in this island, though the short time did not admit of my ascertaining this for a certainty. Here also is found the gold they wear fastened in their noses. But, in order not to lose time, I intend to go and see if I can find the island of Cipango. Now, as it is night, all the natives have gone on shore with their canoes."

SUNDAY, 14TH OF OCTOBER

"At dawn I ordered the ship's boat and the boats of the caravels to be got ready, and I went along the coast of the island to the N.N.E., to see the other side, which was on the other side to the east, and also to see the villages. Presently I saw two or three, and the people all came to the shore, calling out and giving thanks to God. Some of them brought us water, others came with food, and when they saw that I did not want to land, they got into the sea, and came swimming to us. We understood that they asked us if we had come from heaven. One old man came into the boat, and others cried out, in loud voices, to all the men and women, to come and see the men who had come from heaven, and to bring them to eat and drink. Many came, including women, each bringing something, giving thanks to God, throwing themselves on the ground and shouting to us to come on shore. But I was afraid to land, seeing an extensive

reef of rocks which surrounded the island, with deep water between it and the shore forming a port large enough for as many ships as there are in Christendom, but with a very narrow entrance. It is true that within this reef there are some sunken rocks, but the sea has no more motion than the water in a well. In order to see all this I went this morning, that I might be able to give a full account to your Highnesses, and also where a fortress might be established. I saw a piece of land which appeared like an island, although it is not one, and on it there were six houses. It might be converted into an island in two days, though I do not see that it would be necessary, for these people are very simple as regards the use of arms, as your Highnesses will see from the seven that I caused to be taken, to bring home and learn our language and return; unless your Highnesses should order them all to be brought to Castile, or to be kept as captives on the same island; for with fifty men they can all be subjugated and made to do what is required of them. Close to the above peninsula there are gardens of the most beautiful trees I ever saw, and with leaves as green as those of Castile in the month of April and May, and much water. I examined all that port, and afterwards I returned to the ship and made sail. I saw so many islands that I hardly knew how to determine to which I should go first. Those natives I had with me said, by signs, that there were so many that they could not be numbered, and they gave the names of more than a hundred. At last I looked out for the largest, and resolved to shape a course for it, and so I did. It will be distant five leagues from this of *San Salvador*, and the others some more, some less. All are very flat, and all are inhabited. The natives make war on each other, although these are very simple-minded and handsomely-formed people."

Letter of Columbus to Luis de Santangel

Luis de Santangel, to whom Columbus wrote a letter dated February 15, 1493, had been very interested in Columbus's voyage and had helped to finance the project. Columbus's original letter was written in Spanish and was first published in Latin in April 1493. The Latin publication enabled many Europeans to read of his voyage for the first time.*

*Letter from Columbus to Luis de Santangel in J. F. Jameson (ed.), ORIGINAL NARRATIVES OF EARLY AMERICAN HISTORY, Vol. I, Charles Scribner's Sons, 1906.

Sir:

As I know that you will have pleasure from the great victory which our Lord hath given me in my voyage, I write you this, by which you shall know that in thirty-three days I passed over to the Indies with the fleet which the most illustrious King and Queen, our Lords, gave me; where I found very many islands peopled with inhabitants beyond number. And, of them all, I have taken possession for their Highnesses, with proclamation and the royal standard displayed.... To the first which I found, I gave the name Sant Salvador, in commemoration of His High Majesty, who marvellously hath given all this: the Indians call it Guanahani ... there are many havens on the sea-coast; incomparable with any others that I know in Christendom, and plenty of rivers so good and great that it is a marvel. The lands thereof are high, and in it are very many ranges of hills, and most lofty mountains ... all most beautiful in a thousand shapes, and all accessible, and full of trees of a thousand kinds, so lofty that they seem to reach the sky. And I am assured that they never lose their foliage; as may be imagined, since I saw them as green and as beautiful as they are in Spain during May.... In the earth there are many mines of metals; and there is a population of incalculable number.... There could be no believing, without seeing, such harbors as are here, as well as the many and great rivers, and excellent waters, most of which contain gold.... The people of this island, and all the others that I have found and seen ... go naked, men and women.... They have no iron or steel, nor any weapons.... They have no other weapons than the stems of reeds in their seeding state, on the end of which they fix little sharpened stakes ... they are incurably timid. And whether it be a thing of value, or one of little worth, they are straightways content with whatsoever trifle of whatsoever kind may be given them.... I forbade that anything so worthless as fragments of broken platters, and pieces of broken glass should be given them; although when they were able to get such things, they seemed to think they had the best jewel in the world ... they all believe that power and goodness are in the sky, and they believed very firmly that I, with these ships and crews, came from the sky ... they never saw men wearing clothes nor the like of our ships.

They have in all the islands very many canoes, after the manner of rowing-galleys.... They are not so wide, because they are made of a single log of timber, but a galley could not keep up with them in rowing, for their motion is a thing beyond belief....

I hope their highnesses will decide upon for con-

verting them to our holy faith, unto which they are well disposed.

I took possession of a large town which I named the city of Navidad. And I have made fortification there, and a fort, and I have left therein arms and artillery, and provisions for more than a year.....

It seems to me that in all those islands, the men are all content with a single wife; and to their chief or king they give as many as twenty. The women, it appears to me, do more work than the men. Nor have I been able to learn whether they held personal property, for it seemed to me that whatever one had, they all took share of ... nor are they black like those in Guinea, but have flowing hair.

In another island, which they assure me is larger than Espanola, the people have no hair. In this there is incalculable gold; and concerning these and the rest I bring Indians with me as witnesses....

This enough; and thanks to Eternal God our Lord who gives to all those who walk His way, victory over things which seem impossible.

This briefly, in accordance with the facts. Dated, on the caravel, off the Canary Islands, the 15 February of the year 1493.

At your command,
The Admiral

Beginnings of English Settlement—Virginia

One of the most difficult periods of early Virginia history was the so-called starving time in the winter of 1609-1610. Captain John Smith, who tells about this period in the following selection, was the leader of the settlers at Jamestown. Smith left the colony to return to England, and according to him, was greatly missed by his people.*

... Now we all found the losse of Captaine Smith, yea his greatest maligners could now curse his losse, as for come provision and contribution from the Savages, we had nothing but mortall wounds, with clubs and arrowes; as for our Hogs, Hens, Goats, Sheepe, Horse or what lived, our commanders, officers and Savages daily consumed them ... then swords, armes, pieces, or any thing, we traded with the Savages, whose cruell fingers were so oft imbrewed in our blouds, that what by their crueltie, our Governours indiscretion, and losse of our ships, of

_____
*The Generall Historie of Virginia by Captain John Smith.

five hundred within six months after Captaine Smith's departure, there remained not past sixtie men, women and children, most miserable and poore creatures; and those were preserved for the most part, by roots, herbes, acornes, walnuts, berries, now and then a little fish . . . yea, even the very skinnes of our horses. Nay, so great was our famine, that a Savage we slew and buried, the poorer sort tooke him up againe and stewed with roots and herbs. And one amongst the rest did kill his wife, powdered (salted) her, and had eaten part of her before it was knowne; for which hee was executed, as hee well deserved: now whether shee was better roasted, boyled, carbonado'd, I know not; but of such a dish as powdered wife I never heard of. This was that time, which still to this day (1624) we call the starving time; it were too vile to say, and scarce to be believed, what we endured. . . .

The Mayflower Compact

The Mayflower Compact, written in 1620, is one of the most important documents in American history. The Pilgrims composed the compact by applying the experience they had gained from operating a democratic church. The Mayflower Compact created a civil political body which would be governed by the members of the community. In a sense, each person who signed this document entered into a covenant with his fellow man which recognized each man's duties, rights, and obligations.

The forme was as followeth.

In the name of God, Amen. We whose names are under-written, the loyall subjects of our dread soveraigne Lord, King James, by the grace of God, of Great Britaine, Franc, and Ireland king, defender of the faith, etc., haveing undertaken, for the glorie of God, and advancemente of the Christian faith, and honour of our king and countrie, a voyage to plant the first colonie in the Northerne parts of Virginia, doe by these presents solemnly and mutualy in the presence of God, and one of another, covenant and combine our selves togeather into a civill body politick, for our better ordering and preservation and furtherance of the ends aforesaid; and by vertue hearof to enacte, constitute, and frame such just and equall lawes, ordinances, acts, constitutions, and offices, from time to time, as shall be thought most

meete and convenient for the generall good of the Colonie, unto which we promise all due submission and obedience. In witnes wherof we have hereunder subscribed our names at Cap-Codd the 11. of November, in the year of the raigne of our soveraigne lord, King James, of England, France, and Ireland the eighteenth, and of Scotland the fiftie fourth. Anº. Dom. 1620.

Hardships of the First Winter at Plymouth

The Pilgrims' first winter at Plymouth in 1621 was almost disastrous. According to an account written by Governor William Bradford entitled "Bradford's History of Plymouth Plantation," part of which is reprinted here, only six or seven people remained free of sickness or death.*

But that which was most sadd and lamentable was, that in 2. or 3. moneths time halfe of their company dyed, espetialy in Jan: and February, being the depth of winter, and wanting houses and other comforts; being infected with the scurvie and other diseases, which this long vioage and their inacomodate condition had brought upon them; so as ther dyed some times 2. or 3. of a day, in the foresaid time; that of 100. and odd persons, scarce 50. remained. And of these in the time of most distres, ther was but 6. or 7. sound persons, who, to their great comendations be it spoken, spared no pains, night nor day, but with abundance of toyle and hazard of their owne health, fetched them woode, made them fires, drest them meat, made their beads, washed their lothsome cloaths, cloathed and uncloathed them; in a word, did all the homly and necessarie offices for them which dainty and quesie stomacks cannot endure to hear named; and all this willingly and cherfully, without any grudging in the least, shewing herein their true love unto their freinds and bretheren. A rare example and worthy to be remembred. Tow of these 7. were Mr. William Brewster, ther reverend Elder, and Myles Standish, ther Captein and military comander, unto whom my selfe, and many others, were much beholden in our low and sicke condition. And yet the Lord so upheld these persons, as in this generall calamity they were not at all infected either with sicknes, or lamnes. And what I have said of

---

Hardships and Many Deaths in the First Winter by William Bradford.

these, I may say of many others who dyed in this generall vissitation, and others yet living, that whilst they had health, yea, or any strength continuing, they were not wanting to any that had need of them. And I doute not but their recompence is with the Lord.

Instructions to the Colonists by Lord Baltimore

Although the colony of Maryland was founded as a haven for Catholics, Lord Baltimore wanted Protestants to have full equality in his colony. His tolerance is apparent in his instructions to the colonists in 1633. He directed Catholic settlers to be silent on matters of religion on both land and sea.

Instructions 13 Novem: 1633 directed by the Right Honoᵇˡᵉ Cecilius Lo: Baltimore and Lord of the Provinces of Mary Land and Avalon unto his well beloved Brother Leo: Calvert Esqʳ his Lopˢ Deputy Governor of his province of Mary Land and unto Jerom Hawley and Thomas Cornwaleys Esqrs. his Lopปˢ Commissioners for the government of the said Province.

1. INPRI: His LOPP requires his said Governor and Commissioners thᵗ in their voyage to Mary Land they be very carefull to preserve unity and peace amongst all the passengers on Shipp-board, and that they suffer no scandall nor offence to be given to any of the Protestants, whereby any just complaint may heereafter be made, by them, in Virginea or in England, and that for that end, they cause all Acts of Romane Catholique Religion to be done as privately as may be, and that they instruct all the Romane Catholiques to be silent upon all occasions of discourse concerning matters of Religion; and that the said Governor and Commissioners treate the Protestants wᵗʰ as much mildness and favor as Justice will permitt. And this to be observed at Land as well as at Sea.

Form of Indenture of a Servant

The following selection is the prescribed form for a contract to be made with indentured servants. It was drawn up by Lord Baltimore and published in a pamphlet in 1635 entitled "A Relation of Maryland."

The form is similar to those of other colonies and the pamphlet was an advertisement for those interested in coming to Maryland.

THE FORM OF BINDING A SERVANT.

THIS INDENTURE made the   day of   in the   yeere of our Soveraigne Lord King Charles, etc. betweene of the one party, and on the other party, Witnesseth, that the said   doth hereby covenant promise, and grant, to and with the said   his Executors and Assignes, to serve him from the day of the date hereof, until his first and next arrivall in Maryland; and after for and during the tearme of   yeeres, in such service and imployment, as the said   or his assignes shall there imploy him, according to the custome of the Countrey in the like kind. In consideration whereof, the said   doth promise and grant, to and with the said   to pay for his passing, and to find him with Meat, Drinke, Apparell and Lodging, with other necessaries during the said terme; and at the end of the said terme, to give him one whole yeeres provision of Corne, and fifty acres of Land, according to the order of the countrey. In witnesse whereof, the said   hath hereunto put his hand and seale, the day and yeere above written.

Sealed and delivered in
the presence of

The usuall terme of binding a servant, is for five yeers; but for any artificer, or one that shall deserve more then ordinary, the Adventurer shall doe well to shorten that time, and adde encouragements of another nature (as he shall see cause) rather then to want such usefull men.

Puritan Government

John Winthrop (1588-1649) was elected governor of the Massachusetts Bay Colony in 1629 and arrived with his party in Boston the following year. There was a close relationship between church and state in the Bay Colony which was ruled by a small aristocratic group. There was no room for democracy in the Bay Colony. When Winthrop spoke of liberty in his journal in 1645, it was the liberty to obey both magistrates and ministers.*

...The great questions that have troubled the country, are about the authority of the magistrates and the liberty of the people. It is yourselves who have called us to this office; and being called by you, we have our authority from God, in way of an ordinance, such as hath the image of God eminently stamped upon it, the contempt and violation whereof hath been vindicated with examples of divine vengeance. I entreat you to consider that when you choose magistrates, you take them from among yourselves, men subject to like passions as you are. Therefore, when you see infirmities in us, you should reflect upon your own; and that would make you bear the more with us, and not be severe censurers of the failings of your magistrates, when you have continual experience of the like infirmities in yourselves and others. We account him a good servant who breaks not his covenant. The covenant between you and us is the oath you have taken of us, which is to this purpose, that we shall govern you and judge your causes by the rules of God's laws and our own, according to our best skill. When you agree with a workman to build you a ship or house, etc., he undertakes as well for his skill as for his faithfulness, for it is his profession, and you pay him for both. But when you call one to be a magistrate, he doth not profess nor undertake to have sufficient skill for that office, nor can you furnish him with gifts, etc.; therefore you must run the hazard of his skill and ability. But if he fail in faithfulness, which by his oath he is bound unto, that he must answer for. If it fall out that the case be clear to common apprehension and the rule clear also, if he transgress here, the error is not in the skill but in the evil of the will; it must be required of him. But if the case be doubtful or the rule doubtful to men of such understanding and parts as your magistrates are, if your magistrates should err here, yourselves must bear it.

For the other point concerning liberty, I observe a great mistake in the country about that. There is a twofold liberty—natural (I mean as our nature is now corrupt), and civil or federal. The first is common to man, with beasts and other creatures. By this, man as he stands in relation to man simply, hath liberty to do what he lists; it is a liberty to evil as well as to good. This liberty is incompatible and inconsistent with authority, and cannot endure the least restraint of the most just authority. The exercise and maintaining of this liberty makes men grow more evil and in time to be worse than brute beasts: *omnes sumus licentia deteriores*. This is that great enemy of truth and peace, that wild beast, which all the ordinances of God are bent against to restrain and subdue it. The other kind of liberty I call civil or federal; it may also be termed moral, in reference to the covenant between God and man in the moral law, and the politic covenants and constitutions amongst men themselves. This liberty is the proper end and object of authority and cannot subsist without it; and it is a liberty to that only which is good, just, and honest. This liberty you are to stand for, with the hazard not only of your goods, but of your lives, if need be. Whatsoever crosseth this is not authority, but a distemper thereof. This liberty is maintained and exercised in a way of subjection to authority; it is of the same kind of liberty wherewith Christ hath made us free. The woman's own choice makes such a man her husband; yet being so chosen, he is her lord, and she is to be subject to him, yet in a way of liberty, not of bondage; and a true wife accounts her subjection her honor and freedom, and would not think her condition safe and free but in her subjection to her husband's authority. Such is the liberty of the church under the authority of Christ, her king and husband; his yoke is so easy and sweet to her as a bride's ornaments; and if through frowardness or wantonness, etc., she shake it off at any time, she is at no rest in her spirit until she take it up again; and whether her lord smiles upon her and embraceth her in his arms, or whether he frowns or rebukes, or smites her, she apprehends the sweetness of his love in all, and is refreshed, supported, and instructed by every such dispensation of his authority over her. On the other side, ye know who they are that complain of this yoke and say, let us break their bands, etc., we will not have this man to rule over us. Even so, brethren, it will be between you and your magistrates. If you stand for your natural, corrupt liberties and will do what is good in your own eyes, you will not endure the least weight of authority, but will murmur, and oppose, and be always striving to shake off that yoke. But if you will be satisfied to enjoy such civil and lawful liberties, such as Christ allows you, then will you quietly and cheerfully submit unto that authority which is set over you, in all the administrations of it, for your good. Wherein, if we fail at any time, we hope we shall be willing, by God's assistance, to hearken to good advice from any of you or in any other way of God; so shall your liberties be preserved, in upholding the honor and power of authority amongst you.

---

*John Winthrop, THE WAY OF THE CHURCHES OF CHRIST IN NEW ENGLAND, 1645.

Puritan Religious Ideals

Just as John Winthrop was the civil advocate of theocratic authority in the Bay Colony, John Cotton (1584-1652) was the spokesman for the clergy. Cotton defended Calvinism against both Roger Williams and Anne Hutchinson and won both times. The following selection is from *The Way of Life* written by Cotton in 1641. It defines a Christian's duties to both church and state.*

We are now to speak of living by faith in our outward and temporal life; now our outward and temporal life is twofold which we live in the flesh. It is either a civil or a natural life, for both these lives we live; and they are different the one from the other. Civil life is that whereby we live as members of this or that city or town or commonwealth, in this or that particular vocation and calling. Natural life I call that by which we do live this bodily life; I mean, by which we live a life of sense, by which we eat and drink, by which we go through all conditions, from our birth to our grave, by which we live and move and have our being. And now both these a justified person lives by faith. To begin with the former:

A true believing Christian, a justified person, he lives in his vocation by his faith.

Not only my spiritual life but even my civil life in this world, all the life I live, is by the faith of the Son of God. He exempts no life from the agency of his faith; whether he live as a Christian man or as a member of this or that church or commonwealth, he doth it all by the faith of the Son of God.

Now for opening this point, let me show you what are those several acts of faith which it puts forth about our occasions and vocations that so we may live in God's sight therein.

First, faith draws the heart of a Christian to live in some warrantable calling. As soon as ever a man begins to look towards God and the ways of his grace, he will not rest till he find out some warrantable calling and employment. An instance you have in the prodigal son, that after he had received and spent his portion in vanity, and when being pinched, he came home to himself, and coming home to his father, the very next thing after confession and repentance of his sin, the very next petition he makes is, Make me one of thy hired servants; next after desire of pardon of sin, then, Put me into some calling though it be but of an hired servant, wherein he may bring in God any service. A Christian would no sooner have his sin

*John Cotton, THE HISTORY OF NEW ENGLAND, ed. by James Savage, 2 vols., 1825-1826.

pardoned than his estate to be settled in some good calling, though not as a mercenary slave; but he would offer it up to God as a free-will offering. He would have his condition and heart settled in God's peace but his life settled in a good calling, though it be but of a day laborer yet make me as one that may do thee some service. Paul makes it a matter of great thankfulness to God that he had given him ability and put him in place where he might do him service (I Tim. 1.12). And in the law, they were counted unclean beasts that did not divide the hoof into two (Lev. 11.3). Therefore the camel, though he chewed the cud, yet because he did not divide the hoof, he was counted unclean; and God by the beasts did signify to us sundry sorts of men, who were clean, who not, as you may see in Peter's vision in Acts 10. It shows you then that it is only a clean person that walks with a divided hoof, that sets one foot in his general and the other in his particular calling. He strikes with both; he serves both God and man, else he is an unclean beast. If he have no calling but a general or if no calling but a particular, he is an unclean creature; but now as soon as ever faith purifies the heart, it makes us clean creatures (Acts 15.9); and our callings do not interfere one upon another, but both go an end evenly together. He drives both these plows at once; *as God hath called every man, so let him walk* (I Cor. 7.19, 20). This is the clean work of faith he would have some employment to fill the head and hand with.

* * *

Secondly, another work of faith, about a man's vocation and calling, when faith hath made choice of a warrantable calling, then he depends upon God for the quickening and sharpening of his gifts in that calling, and yet depends not upon his gifts for the going through his calling but upon God that gave him those gifts; yea, he depends on God for the use of them in his calling. Faith saith not, Give me such a calling and turn me loose to it; but faith looks up to heaven for skill and ability. Though strong and able, yet it looks at all its abilities but as a dead work, as like braided wares in a shop, as such as will be lost and rust unless God refresh and renew breath in them. And then if God do breathe in his gifts, he depends not upon them for the acting his work but upon God's blessing in the use of his gifts. Though he have never so much skill and strength, he looks at it as a dead work unless God breathe in him; and he looks not at his gifts as breathed only on by God, as able to do the work, unless also he be followed by God's blessing. *Blessed be the Lord my strength, that teacheth my hands to war, and my fingers to fight* (Psal. 44.1). He had been trained up to skill that way, yet he rests only in God's teaching of him (Psal. 18.32, 33, 34). *It is the Lord that girds me with strength;* he puts strength into his hands, so that a *bow of steel is broken with my arms.* And therefore it was that when he went against Goliath, though he had before found good success in his combats with the lion and the bear, yet he saith not, I have made my part good enough with them, and so shall I do with this man. No, but this is the voice of faith; *the Lord my God that delivered me out of their hands, he will deliver me out of the hand of this Philistine;* he that gave me strength and skill at that time, he is the same, *his hand is not shortened.* And then what is this Philistine more than one of them (I Sam. 17.37)? And so when he comes in Goliah's presence and looks in his face, he tells him he comes to him *in the name of the Lord of Hosts;* and he comes not only in the Lord's name, but he *looks up to him for skill and strength to help;* and therefore saith ver. 40, *The Lord will close thee in my hands,* so that by his own strength shall no flesh prevail. *It is in vain,* saith faith, *to rise early, and go to bed late, but it is God that gives his beloved rest* (Psal. 127.1, 2, 3; Prov. 3.5, 6). The strongest Christian is never more foiled than when he goes forth in strength of gifts received and his own dexterity.

Thirdly, we live by faith in our vocations, in that faith, *in serving God, serves men, and in serving men, serves God.* The apostle sweetly describes it in the calling of servants (Eph. 6.5 to 8); *not with eye service as men-pleasers, but as the servants of Christ, doing the will of God from the heart with good will, as unto the Lord, and not unto men,* not so much man or only man, but chiefly the Lord, so that this is the work of every Christian man in his calling. Even then when he serves man, he serves the Lord; he doth the work set before him, and he doth it sincerely and faithfully so as he may give account for it; and he doth it heavenly and spiritually; *He uses the world as if he used it not* (I Cor. 7.31). This is not the thing his heart is set upon, he looks for greater matters than these things can reach him, he doth not so much look at the world as at heaven. And therefore that which follows upon this, he doth it all comfortably though he meet with little encouragements from man, though the more faithful service he doth, the less he is accepted; whereas an unbelieving heart would be discontented that he can find no acceptance, but all he doth is taken in the worst part; but now if faith be working and stirring, he will say, *I pass very little to be judged by you, or by man's judgment* (I Cor. 4.3).I pass little what you say or what you do; God knows what I have done, and so his spirit is satisfied (I Thess. 2.6); *we were tender over you, as a nurse over her child;* we wrought not for wages nor for the praise of you; if so, we had not been the servants of Christ. A man therefore that serves Christ in serving of men, he doth his work sincerely as in God's presence, and as one that hath an heavenly business in hand, and therefore comfortably as knowing God approves of his way and work.

Fourthly, another act of faith about a man's vocation is this: It encourageth a man in his calling to the most homeliest and difficultest and most dangerous things his calling can lead and expose himself to; if faith apprehend this or that to be the way of my calling, it encourages me to it, though it be never so homely and difficult and dangerous. Take you a carnal, proud heart; and if his calling lead him to some homely business, he can by no means embrace it; such homely employments a carnal heart knows not how to submit unto. But now faith having put us into a calling, if it require some homely employment, it encourageth us to it. He considers, It is my calling, and therefore he goes about it freely; and though never so homely, he doth it as a work of his calling. (Luke 15.19) *Make me one of thy hired servants.* A man of his rank and breeding was not wonted to hired servile work, but the same faith that made him desirous to be in a calling made him stoop to any work his calling led him to; there is no work too hard or too homely for him, for faith is conscious that it hath done most base drudgery for Satan. No lust of pride or what else so insolent but our base hearts could be content to serve the Devil and nature in it; and therefore what drudgery can be too homely for me to do for God? (Phil. 2.5, 7) *Let the same mind be in you that was in Christ Jesus, he made himself of no reputation;* he stood not upon it that he was born of God and equal to the Most High; but he made himself a servant, and of no reputation, and so to serve God and save men; and when his Father called him to it, he stooped to a very low employment, rose up from supper and girded himself with a towel and washed his disciples' feet (John 13). They thought it was a service too homely for him to do, but he tells them that even they ought thus to serve one another. So faith is ready to embrace any homely service his calling leads him to, which a carnal heart would blush to be seen in; a faithful heart is never squeamish in this case, for repentance will make a man revenge himself upon himself in respect of the many homely services he hath done for Satan; and so faith encourageth us to the most difficult and homely business. (Ezra 10.4) *It is a great thing* thou art now about, yet *arise and be doing, for the matter belongs to thee.* Yea, and though sometimes the work be more dangerous, yet if a man be called to it, faith dares not shrink. It was an hard point that Herod was put upon: either now he must be profane or discover his hypocrisy. Now therefore, John dischargeth his conscience; and though it was dangerous for him to be so plain, yet faith encourageth him to it. If it appear to be his calling, faith doth not pick and choose as carnal reason will do.

Fifthly, another act of faith by which a Christian man lives in his vocation is that faith casts all the failings and burthens of his calling upon the Lord; that is the proper work of faith; it rolls and casts all upon him.

* * *

Sixthly, faith hath another act about a man's vocation, and that is, it takes all successes that befall him in his calling with moderation; he equally bears good and evil successes as God shall dispense them to him. Faith frames the heart to moderation; be they good or evil, it rests satisfied in God's gracious dispensation; *I have learned in what estate soever I am, therewith to be content* (Phil. 4.11, 12). This he had learned to do: if God prosper him, he had learned not to be puffed up; and if he should be exposed to want, he could do it without murmuring. It is the same act of unbelief that makes a man murmur in crosses which puffs him up in prosperity. Now faith is like a poise: it keeps the heart in an equal frame; whether matters fall out well or ill, faith takes them much what alike; faith moderates the frame of a man's spirit on both sides.

Seventhly, the last work which faith puts forth about a man's calling is this: faith with boldness resigns up his calling into the hands of God or man; whenever God calls a man to lay down his calling when his work is finished, herein the sons of God far exceed the sons of men. Another man when his calling comes to be removed from him, he is much ashamed and much afraid; but if a Christian man be to forgo his calling, he lays it down with comfort and boldness in the sight of God and man.

* * *

The American Indian
Seen Through European Eyes

This reading describes Indian life in America as observed by two Dutchmen in 1644 and 1655. The two Dutchmen were among the first Europeans to write about the Indian in general and the Mohawk tribes of New York in particular. Descriptions of Indian dress, physical appearance, social behavior, war practices, duties of daily life, and the manner in which the Indians buried their dead are included.[*]

THE DRESS OF THE MOHAWKS AND THEIR WOMEN

The people and Indians here in this country are like us Dutchmen in body and stature; some of them have well formed features, bodies and limbs; they all have black hair and eyes, but their skin is yellow. In summer they go naked, having only their private parts covered with a patch. The children and young folks to ten, twelve and fourteen years of age go stark naked. In winter, they hang about them simply an undressed deer or bear or panther skin; or they take some beaver and otter skins, wild cat, raccoon, martin, otter, mink, squirrel or such like skins, which are plenty in this country, and sew some of them to others, until it is a square piece, and that is then a garment for them; or they buy of us Dutchmen two and a half ells of duffel, and that they hang simply about them, just as it was torn off, without sewing it, and walk away with it. They look at themselves constantly, and think they are very fine. They make themselves stockings and also shoes of deer skin, or they take leaves of their corn, and plait them together and use them for shoes. The women, as well as the men, go with their heads bare. The women let their hair grow very long, and tie it together a little, and let it hang down their backs. The men have a long lock of hair hanging down, some on one side of the head, and some on both sides. On the top of their heads they have a streak of hair from the forehead to the neck, about the breadth of three fingers, and this they shorten until it is about two or three fingers long, and it stands right on end like a cock's comb or hog's bristles; on both sides of this cock's comb they cut all the hair short, except the aforesaid locks, and they also leave on the bare places here and there small locks, such as are in sweeping-brushes, and then they are in fine array.

They likewise paint their faces red, blue, etc., and then they look like the Devil himself. They smear their heads with bear's-grease, which they all carry with them for this purpose in a small basket; they say they do it to make their hair grow better and to prevent their having lice. When they travel, they take with them some of their maize, a kettle, a wooden bowl, and a spoon; these they pack up and hang on their backs. Whenever they are hungry, they forth-

---

[*]*The Dress of the Mohawks and Their Women* by Rev. Johannes Megapolensis, Jr. and *Description of the Indians Near Fort Amsterdam* by David Pietersz de Vries in J. F. Jameson (ed.), ORIGINAL NARRATIVES OF EARLY AMERICAN HISTORY, Vol. IX, Charles Scribner's Sons, 1909.

with make a fire and cook; they can get fire by rubbing pieces of wood against one another, and that very quickly.

They generally live without marriage; and if any of them have wives, the marriage continues no longer than seems good to one of the parties, and then they separate, and each takes another partner. I have seen those who had parted, and afterwards lived a long time with others, leave these again, seek their former partners, and again be one pair. . . .

The women, when they have been delivered, go about immediately afterwards, and be it ever so cold, they wash themselves and the young child in the river or the snow. They will not lie down (for they say that if they did they would soon die), but keep going about. They are obliged to cut wood, to travel three or four leagues with the child; in short, they walk, they stand, they work, as if they had not lain in, and we cannot see that they suffer any injury by it; and we sometimes try to persuade our wives to lie-in so, and that the way of lying-in in Holland is a mere fiddle-faddle. The men have great authority over their concubines, so that if they do anything which does not please and raises their passion, they take an axe and knock them in the head, and there is an end of it. The women are obliged to prepare the land, to mow, to plant, and do everything; the men do nothing, but hunt, fish, and make war upon their enemies. They are very cruel towards their enemies in time of war; for they first bite off the nails of the fingers of their captives, and cut off some joints, and sometimes even whole fingers; after that, the captives are forced to sing and dance before them stark naked; and finally, they roast their prisoners dead before a slow fire for some days, and then eat them up. . . .

Our Mahakas carry on great wars against the Indians of Canada, on the River Saint Lawrence, and take many captives, and sometimes there are French Christians among them. Last year, our Indians got a great booty from the French on the River Saint Lawrence, and took three Frenchmen, one of whom was a Jesuit. They killed one, but the Jesuit (whose left thumb was cut off, and all the nails and parts of his fingers were bitten,) we released, and sent him to France by a yacht which was going to our country. They spare all the children from ten to twelve years old, and all the women whom they take in war, unless the women are very old, and then they kill them too. Though they are so very cruel to their enemies, they are very friendly to us, and we have no dread of them. We go with them into the woods, we meet with each other, sometimes at an hour or two's walk from any houses, and think no more about it than as if we met with a Christian. They sleep by us, too, in our chambers before our beds. I have had eight at once lying and sleeping upon the floor near my bed, for it is their custom to sleep simply on the bare ground, and to have only a stone or a bit of wood under their heads. In the evening, they go to bed very soon after they have supped; but early in the morning, before day begins to break, they are up again. They are very slovenly and dirty; they wash neither their face nor hands, but let all remain upon their yellow skin, and look like hogs. Their bread is Indian corn beaten to pieces between two stones, of which they make a cake, and bake it in the ashes: their other victuals are venison, turkies, hares, bears, wild cats, their own dogs, etc. . . .

DESCRIPTION OF THE INDIANS NEAR FORT AMSTERDAM

The Indians below here are also tolerably stout, have black hair, with a long lock, which they braid and let hang on one side of the head. The hair is shorn on the top of the head like a cock's-comb, . . . Their disposition is bad. They are very revengeful; resembling the Italians. Their clothing is a coat of beaver-skins over the body, with the fur inside in winter, and outside in summer; they have, also, sometimes a bear's hide, or a coat of the skins of wild cats, or *hesspanen,* which is an animal almost as hairy as a wild cat, and is also very good to eat. I have frequently eaten it, and found it very tender. They also wear coats of turkey's feathers, which they know how to plait together; but since our Netherland nation has traded here, they trade their beavers for duffels cloth, which we give for them, and which they find more suitable than the beavers, as they consider it better for the rain; and take two and a half in length of duffels, which is nine and a half quarters wide. Their pride is to paint their faces strangely with red or black lead, so that they look like fiends. They are then valiant; yea, they say they are *Mannette,* the Devil himself. Some of the women are very well-featured, and of tall stature. Their hair hangs loose from their head; they are very foul and dirty; they sometimes paint their faces, and sometimes draw a black ring around their eyes. When they wish to cleanse themselves of their foulness, they go in the autumn, when it begins to grow cold, and make, away off, near a running brook, a small oven, large enough for three or four men to lie in it. In making it they first take twigs of trees, and then cover them tight with clay, so that smoke cannot escape. This being done, they take a parcel of stones, which they heat in a fire, and then put in the oven, and when they think that it is sufficiently hot, they take the stones out again, and go and lie in it, men and women, boys and girls, and come out so perspiring, that every hair has a drop of sweat on it. In this state they plunge into the cold water; saying that it is healthy, but I let its healthfulness pass; they then become entirely clean, and are more attractive than before. The girls consider themselves to have arrived at womanhood when they begin to have their monthly terms, and as soon as they have them, they go and disguise themselves with a garment, which they throw over their body drawing it over the head so that one can barely see their eyes, and run off for two or three months, lamenting that they must lose their virginity; but for all that they do not omit their diversions at night, or other unseasonable time. This period being over, they throw away their disguise, and deck themselves with a quantity of *zeewan* upon the body, head and neck; they then go and sit in some place, in company with some squaws, showing they are up for a bargain. Whoever courts best and gives the most *zeewan* takes her home with him, and remains with her sometimes three or four months, and then goes with another; sometimes a single month, according as they are inclined to each other....

IN WHAT MANNER THEY BURY THEIR DEAD.

They make a large grave, and line it inside with boughs of trees, in which they lay the corpse, so that no earth can touch it. They then cover this with clay, and form the grave, seven or eight feet high, in the shape of a sugar-loaf, and place palisades around it. I have frequently seen the wife of the deceased come daily to the grave, weeping and crying, creeping around it with extended body, and grieving for the death of her husband. The oldest wife by whom he has had children does this; if he has also had a young wife, she does not make much ado about it, but looks out for another husband. They give a party when any one is dead in the house. I have seen at the North, great multitudes of savages assembled, who had collected together the bones of their ancestors, cleaned them, and bound them up in small bundles. They dig a square grave, the size and length of the person, and over it erect four pillars, which they cover with the bark of trees ... they set a time when they will bury the body, when all the friends will have a great gathering, and bring ample supplies of provisions, accordingly as is prescribed by their village, that a great festival is to be held, with frolic and dancing. This festival continues some ten days, during which time their friends come from other nations on all sides, in order to see it held, and the accompanying ceremonies, which are attended with great expense. Under cover of these ceremonies, dances, feasts, and meetings, they contract new alliances of friendship with their neighbors; saying, that as the bones of their ancestors and friends are together in the little bundles (using this as a figure), so may their bones be together in the same place, and that as long as their lives shall last, they ought to be united in friendship and concord, as were their ancestors and friends, without being able to be separated from each other, like as the bones of the ancestors and friends of each other are mingled together. One of them—their chief or their devil-hunter—delivers much speech over the bones (saying), "that if they remain thus united, their enemies can have no power over them." They then bury the bones in the grave, with a parcel of *zeewan*, and with arrows, kettles, knives, paper, wicks, and other knick-knacks, which are held in great esteem by them, and cover them with earth, and place palisades around them as before related. Such is the custom on the coast in regard to the dead. The chief doctrine held among them is the belief in the immortality of the soul by some. Others are in doubt of this, but not far from it, saying, when they die they go to a place where they sing like the ravens; but this singing is entirely different from the singing of the angels.

Surrender of New Netherland

In September 1664, the city and colony of New York began and that of New Netherland ended. The English sent a military force to New Netherland and demanded that the territory be turned over to them. After reviewing their situation, the Dutch decided to surrender peacefully. The following selection is a letter written by the colonial town council of Amsterdam explaining to the Dutch directors the reasons for the surrender.*

Right Honorable Prudent Lords, the Lords Directors of the Honorable West India Company, Department of Amsterdam:

Right Honorable Lords:

We, your Honors' loyal, sorrowful and desolate subjects, cannot neglect nor keep from relating the event, which through God's pleasure thus unexpectedly happened to us in consequence of your Honors' neglect and forgetfulness of your promise—to wit, the arrival here, of late, of four King's frigates from England, sent hither by His Majesty and his brother, the Duke of York, with commission to reduce not only this place, but also the whole New

---

*Surrender of New Netherland from the Minutes of the Court of Burgomasters and Schepens in J. F. Jameson (ed.), ORIGINAL NARRATIVES OF EARLY AMERICAN HISTORY, Vol. IX, Charles Scribner's Sons, 1909.

Netherland under His Majesty's authority, whereunto they brought with them a large body of soldiers, provided with considerable ammunition. On board one of the frigates were about four hundred and fifty as well soldiers as seamen, and the others in proportion.

The frigates being come together in front of Najac in the Bay, Richard Nicolls, the admiral, who is ruling here at present as Governor, sent a letter to our Director General, communicating therein the cause of his coming and his wish. On this unexpected letter the General sent for us to determine what was to be done herein. Whereupon it was resolved and decided to send some commissioners thither, to argue the matter with the General and his three commissioners, who were so sent for this purpose twice, but received no answer, than that they were not come here to dispute about it, but to execute their order and commission without fail, either peaceably or by force, and if they had anything to dispute about it, it must be done with His Majesty of England, as we could do nothing here in the premises. Three days' delay was demanded for consultation; that was duly allowed. But meanwhile they were not idle; they approached with their four frigates, two of which passed in front of the fort, the other anchored about Nooten Island and with five companies of soldiers encamped themselves at the ferry, opposite this place, together with a newly raised company of horse and a party of new soldiers, both from the North and from Long Island, mostly our deadly enemies, who expected nothing else than pillage, plunder and bloodshed, as men could perceive by their cursing and talking, when mention was made of a capitulation.

Finally, being then surrounded, we saw little means of deliverance; we resolved what ought to be here done, and after we had well enquired into our strength and had found it to be full fifteen hundred souls strong in this place, but of whom not two hundred and fifty men are capable of bearing arms exclusive of the soldiers, who were about one hundred and fifty strong, wholly unprovided with powder both in the city and in the fort; yea, not more than six hundred pounds were found in the fort besides seven hundred pounds unserviceable; also because the farmers, the third man of whom was called out, refused, we with the greater portion of the inhabitants considered it necessary to remonstrate with our Director General and Council, that their Honors might consent to a capitulation, whereunto we labored according to our duty and had much trouble; and laid down and considered all the difficulties, which should arise from our not being able to resist such an enemy, as they besides could receive a much greater force than they had under their command.

The Director General and Council at length consented thereunto, whereto commissioners were sent to the admiral, who notified him that it was resolved to come to terms in order to prevent the shedding of blood, if a good agreement could be concluded.

Six persons were commissioned on each side for this purpose to treat on this matter, as they have done and concluded in manner as appears by articles annexed. How that will result, time shall tell.

Meanwhile since we have no longer to depend on your Honors' promises of protection, we, with all the poor, sorrowing and abandoned commonalty here, must fly for refuge to Almighty God, not doubting but He will stand by us in this sorely afflicting conjuncture and no more depart from us: And we remain

Your sorrowful and abandoned subjects,
 PIETER TONNEMAN,
 PAULUS LEENDERZEN VAN DER GRIFT,
 CORNELIS STEENWYCK,
 JACOB BACKER,
 TYMOTHEUS GABRY,
 ISAACK GREVENRAAT,
 NICOLAAS DE MEYER.

Done in Jorck [York] heretofore named Amsterdam in New Netherland Anno 1664 the 16th September.

The Second Treatise of Government

In 1690, the English scholar John Locke wrote *Two Treatises of Government* in defense of the Glorious Revolution of 1688. Locke's *Second Treatise of Government* explained the basis of government and the conditions which justified revolution. Nearly a century later, many of Locke's ideas influenced the thinking of American colonists.*

OF THE STATE OF NATURE

To understand political power right, and derive it from its original, we must consider what state all men are naturally in, and that is, a state of perfect freedom to order their actions, and dispose of their possessions and persons as they think fit, within the bounds of the law of nature, without asking leave or depending upon the will of any other man.

A *state* also *of equality*, wherein all the power and jurisdiction is reciprocal, no one having more than another, there being nothing more evident than that creatures of the same species and rank, promiscuously

---

*John Locke, THE SECOND TREATISE OF GOVERNMENT, (London, 1690), Old South Leaflet No. 208. Reprinted by courtesy of the Old South Association in Boston.

born to all the same advantages of nature, and the use of the same faculties, should also be equal one amongst another without subordination or subjection, unless the lord and master of them all should, by any manifest declaration of his will, set one above another, and confer on him, by an evident and clear appointment, an undoubted right to dominion and sovereignty. . . .

But though this be *a state of liberty,* yet *it is not a state of license;* though man in that state have an uncontrollable liberty to dispose of his person or possessions, yet he has not liberty to destroy himself, or so much as any creature in his possession, but where some nobler use than its bare preservation calls for it. The *state of nature* has a law of nature to govern it, which obliges every one, and reason, which is that law, teaches all mankind who will but consult it, that being all *equal and independent,* no one ought to harm another in his life, health, liberty or possessions. . . .

OF TYRANNY

As usurpation is the exercise of power which another hath a right to, so *tyranny is the exercise of power beyond right,* which nobody can have a right to; and this is making use of the power any one has in his hands, not for the good of those who are under it, but for his own private, separate advantage. When the governor, however entitled, makes not the law, but his will, the rule, and his commands and actions are not directed to the preservation of the properties of his people, but the satisfaction of his own ambition, revenge, covetousness, or any other irregular passion. . . .

It is a mistake to think this fault is proper only to monarchies. Other forms of government are liable to it as well as that; for wherever the power that is put in any hands for the government of the people and the preservation of their properties is applied to other ends, and made use of to impoverish, harass, or subdue them to the arbitrary and irregular commands of those that have it, there it presently becomes tyranny, whether those that thus use it are one or many. . . .

Wherever law ends, tyranny begins, if the law be transgressed to another's harm; and whosoever in authority exceeds the power given him by the law and makes use of the force he has under his command to compass that upon the subject which the law allows not, ceases in that to be a magistrate, and acting without authority may be opposed, as any other man who by force invades the right of another. This is acknowledged in subordinate magistrates. He

that hath authority to seize my person in the street may be opposed as a thief and a robber if he endeavors to break into my house to execute a writ, notwithstanding that I know he has such a warrant and such a legal authority as will empower him to arrest me abroad. And why this should not hold in the highest, as well as in the most inferior magistrate, I would gladly be informed. Is it reasonable that the eldest brother, because he has the greatest part of his father's estate, should thereby have a right to take away any of his younger brothers' portions? Or, that a rich man, who possessed a whole country, should from thence have a right to seize, when he pleased, the cottage and garden of his poor neighbor? The being rightfully possessed of great power and riches, exceedingly beyond the greatest part of the sons of Adam, is so far from being an excuse, much less a reason for rapine and oppression, which the endamaging another without authority is, that it is a great aggravation of it. . . .

May the *commands,* then, *of a prince be opposed?* May he be resisted, as often as anyone shall find himself aggrieved, and but imagine he has not right done him? This will unhinge and overturn all polities, and instead of government and order, leave nothing but anarchy and confusion.

To this I answer: That *force* is to be opposed to nothing but to *unjust and unlawful force.* Whoever makes any opposition in any other case draws on himself a just condemnation, both from God and man; and so no such danger or confusion will follow, as is often suggested. . . .

OF THE DISSOLUTION OF GOVERNMENTS

To conclude: The *power that every individual gave the society* when he entered into it can never revert to the individuals again, as long as the society lasts, but will always remain in the community; because without this there can be no community—no commonwealth, which is contrary to the original agreement; so also when the society hath placed the legislative in any assembly of men, to continue in them and their successors, with direction and authority for providing such successors, *the legislative can never revert to the people whilst that government lasts;* because, having provided a legislative with power to continue for ever, they have given up their political power to the legislative, and cannot resume it. But if they have set limits to the duration of their legislative, and made this supreme power in any person or assembly only temporary; or else, when, by the miscarriages of those in authority, it is forfeited; upon the forfeiture of their rulers, or at the determination of the time set, *it reverts to the society,* and the people have a right to act as supreme, and continue the legislative in themselves or place it in a new form, or new hands, as they think good.

Letter of Edward Randolph
to the Board of Trade

The letter by Edward Randolph to the British Board of Trade, reprinted here, describes the general situation in South Carolina and particularly the city of Charleston in 1699. At this early period Randolph points out the constant Spanish threat from the south in Florida and the French threat from the Mississippi River Valley in the west. The letter also includes references to a growing business in rice and such naval stores as pitch, tar, turpentine, and lumber for which the Carolinas became well known in later years.

E. Randolph to the Lords of Trade, 16 March, 1698-1699.

May it please yʳ Lordships,

After a dangerous voyage at Sea, I landed at Charles Town, in the Province of So. Carolina, and soon after my arrival, I administered the Oath to Mr. Jos. Blake, one of the Proprietors and Governor of this Province. But he is not allowed of by his Maᵗʸˢ Order in Council to be Govr., the Act of Parlt. for preventing frauds being not taken notice of by the Proprietors.

There are but few settled Inhabitants in this Province, the Lords have taken up vast tracts of land for their own use, as in Colleton County and other places, where the land is most commodious for settlement, which prevents peopling the place, and makes them less capable to preserve themselves. As to their civil Governt., 'tis different from what I have met with in the other Proprieties. Their Militia is not above 1500 Soldiers White men, but have thro' the Province generally 4 Negroes to 1 White man, and not above 1100 families, English and French.

Their Chief Town is Charles Town, and the seat of Govt. in this Province, where the Governor, Council and Triennial Parliamt. set, and their Courts are holden, being above a league distance from the entrance to their harbour mouth, wᶜʰ is barred, and not above 17 foot water at the highest tide, but very difficult to come in. The Harbour is called by the Spaniards, St. George; it lyes 75 leagues to the Northward of St. Augustine, belonging to the Spaniards. It is generally laid down in our English maps to be 2

deg., 45 min., within the southern bounds of this Province. In the year 1686, one hundred Spaniards, wᵗʰ Negroes and Indians, landed at Edistoe, (50 miles to the southward of Charles Town,) and broak open the house of Mr. Joseph Moreton, then Governor of the Province, and carried away Mr. Bowell, his Brother-in-law, prisoner, who was found murdered 2 or 3 days after; they carried away all his money and plate, and 13 slaves, to the value of £1500 sterling, and their plunder to St. Augustine. Two of the Slaves made their escape from thence, and returned to their master. Some time after, Govr. Moreton sent to demand his slaves, but the Govr. of St. Augustine answered it was done without his orders, but to this day keeps them, and says he can't deliver them up wᵗʰout an ordʳ from the King of Spain. About the same time they robbed Mr. Grimball's House, the Sec. of the Province, whilst he attended the Council at Charles Town, and carried away to the value of over £1500 sterlᵍ. They also fell upon a settlement of Scotchmen at Port Royal, where there was not above 25 men in health to oppose them. The Spaniards burnt down their houses, destroyed and carried away all that they had, because (as the Spanᵈˢ pretended) they were settled upon their land, and had they at any time a superior force, they would also destroy this town built upon Ashley and Cooper Rivers. This whole Bay was called formerly St. George's, which they likewise lay claim to. The Inhabitants complained of the wrong done them by the Spaniards to the Lords Proprietors, and humbly prayed them (as I have been truly informed) to represent it to His Maᵗʸ, but they not hearing from the Lord Proprs, fitted out two vessels with 400 stout men, well armed, and resolved to take St. Augustine. But Jas. Colleton came in that time from Barbadoes with a Commission to be Govr., and threatn'd to hang them if they proceeded, whereupon they went on shore very unwillingly. The Spaniards hearing the English were coming upon them for the damages, they left their Town and Castle, and fled into the woods to secure themselves. The truth is, as I have been credibly informed, there was a design on foot to carry on a Trade with the Spaniards.

I find the Inhabitants greatly alarmed upon the news that the French continue their resolution to make a settling at Messasipi River, from [whence] they may come over land to the head of Ashley River wᵗʰout opposition, 'tis not yet known what care the Lords Proprs intend to take for their preservation. Some ingenious gentlemen of this Province (not of the Council) have lately told me the Deputies have talked of makᵍ an Address to the Lords Proprs for relief. But 'tis apparent that all the time of this French War they never sent them one barrel of powder or a pound of lead to help them. They conclude they have no reason to depend upon them for assistance, and are resolved to forsake this Country betimes, if they find the French are settled at Meschasipi, or if upon the death of the King of Spain these Countries fall into the hands of the French, as inevitably they will (if not timely prevented), and return with their families to England or some other place where they may find safety and protection. It was one of the first questions asked by several of the Chief men at my arrival, whether His Ma^ty will please to allow them half pay for 2 or 3 years at furthest, that afterwards they will maintain themselves and families (if they have any) in making Pitch and Tar and planting of Indian Corn. His Majesty will thereby have so many men seasoned to the Country ready for service upon all occasions, five such men will do more service by sea or land then 20 new rais^d men from home, they may be brought hither in the Virginia outward bound ships, 100 or 150 men in a year, till they are made up 1000, it will save the charge of transporting so many another time 2 or 3000 leagues at sea. I heard one of the Council (a great Indian Trader, and has been 600 miles up in the Country west from Charles Town) discourse that the only way to discover the Meschasipi is from this Province by land. He is willing to undertake it if His Ma^ty will please to pay the charge wch will not be above £400 or £500 at most; he intends to take with him 50 white men of this Province and 100 Indians, who live 2 days journey east from the Meschasipi, and questions not but in 5 or 6 months time after he has His Ma^ty's commands and instructions to find out the mouth of it and the true latitude thereof.

The great improvement made in this Province is wholly owing to the industry and labour of the Inhabitants. They have applied themselves to make such commodities as might increase the revenue of the Crown, as Cotton, Wool, Ginger, Indigo, etc. But finding them not to answer the end, they are set upon making Pitch, Tar and Turpentine, and planting rice, and can send over great quantityes yearly, if they had encouragement from England to make it, having about 5,000 Slaves to be employed in that service, upon occasion, but they have lost most of their vessels, which were but small, last war by the French, and some lately by the Spaniards, so that they are not able to send those Commodities to England for a market, neither are sailors here to be had to man their vessels.

I humbly propose that if His Ma^ty will for a time suspend the Duties upon Commodities, and that upon rice also, it will encourage the Planter to fall vigilantly upon making Pitch and Tar, etc., wch the Lords Prop^rs ought to make their principal care to obtain from His Ma^ty, being the only way to draw people to settle in their Province, a place of greatest encouragement to the English Navy in these parts of the world. Charles Town Bay is the safest port for all vessels coming thro' the gulf of Florida in distress, bound from the West Indies to the Northern Plantations; if they miss this place they may perish at sea for want of relief, and having beat upon the coast of New England, New York, or Virginia by a North West Wind in the Winter, be forced to go to Barbadoes if they miss this Bay, where no wind will damage them and all things to be had necessary to refitt them. My Lords, I did formerly present Your Lordships with proposals for supplying England with Pitch and Tar, Masts and all o^r Naval Stores from New England. I observed when I were at York in Septr. last, abundance of Tar brot. down Hudson's River to be sold at New York, as also Turpentine and Tar in great quantities from the Colony of Connecticut. I was told if they had encouragement they could load several Ships yearly for England. But since my arrival here I find I am come into the only place for such commodities upon the Continent of America; some persons have offered to deliver in Charlestown Bay upon their own account 1000 Barrels of Pitch and as much Tar, others greater quantities provided they were paid for it in Charles Town in Lyon Dollars passing here at 5s. p^r piece, Tar at 8s. p^r Barrel, and very good Pitch at 12s. p^r Barrel, and much cheaper if it once became a trade. The season for making those Commodities in this Province being 6 mos. longer than in Virginia and more Northern Plantations, a planter can make more tar in any one year here with 50 slaves than they can do with double the number in those places, their slaves here living at very easy rates and with few clothes.

The inclosed I received from M. Girard, a French Protestant living in Carolina. I find them very industrious and good husbands, but are discouraged because some of them having been many years Inhabitants in this Province are denied the benefit of being Owners and Masters of Vessels, which other the Subjects of His Majesty's Plantations enjoy, besides many of them are made Denizons. If this Place were duly encouraged, it would be the most useful to the Crown of all the Plantations upon the continent of America. I herewith enclose to Your Lordships a Draft of the Town and Castle of St. Augustine, with a short description of it by a Gentleman who has been often there. It's done exactly true, more for service than for show. The Spaniards now, the French, if ever they get it, will prove dangerous neighbours to this Province, a thing not considered nor provided against by the

Lords Proprietors. I am going from hence to Bermuda, with His Ma^tys Commissioners, to administer the Oath to the Govr. of that Island, with a Commission for the Judge and other Officers of the Court of Admiralty erected there, from whence I believe it necessary to hasten to the Bahamas Islands, where a Brigantine belonging to New England was carried in as a wreck. The Master and Sailors being pursued by some persons who had commission from Govr. Webb, believing they were chased by Spaniards, forsook their Vessel and went on shore among the Natives to save their lives.

All which is humbly submitted by

Your Lordship's

Most humble Servant,

ED. RANDOLPH.

William Penn's Laws for Pennsylvania

Francis Daniel Pastorius, a German, became attracted to the philosophy of William Penn. He was one of the first of many Germans to emigrate to Pennsylvania, arriving in Philadelphia in 1683. A leader of the early German settlement, Pastorius founded Germantown, which is today a section of Philadelphia. He was a well-educated man and wrote a great deal, as can be seen in the following selection published in 1700 and entitled: "Circumstantial Geographical Description of the Lately Discovered Province of Pennsylvania, Situated in the Farthest Limits of America, in the Western World." Pastorius writes about Penn's laws for the Province. These laws demonstrated a feeling for godliness, democracy, and freedom of religion.*

CONCERNING THE LAWS OF THE PROVINCE

William Penn established the first [of these] with the concurrence of the public assembly:

1. The members of the council, and then the whole community come together each year upon a certain appointed day and choose their presiding officers and other functionaries by lot, so that none may know who has voted for, or against, him. Thereby is prevented all improper use of money, and likewise the secret enmity of the defeated candidate. And if anyone has conducted himself improperly this year, a better man may be chosen next time.

2. No tax, excise, or other impost may be laid

upon the public without the consent of two-thirds of the council.

3. In order to prevent litigation, law-suits, and quarrelling, a record will be kept, wherein will be registered all estates, mortgages, obligations, and rents. Thus all advocates and attorneys who demand money for their services are discarded.

4 and 5. That no one sect may raise itself above the others, each shall enjoy freedom of conscience, and no one shall be forced to be present at any public services for the worship of God, and no one shall be disturbed in his belief or religion.

6. In order to guard against whatever could tempt the people to frivolity, wantonness, insolence, audacity, ungodliness, and scandalous living, all wordly plays, comedies, games of cards, maskings, all cursing, swearing, lying, bearing of false witness (since an oath is not allowed), scandal-mongering, adultery, lewdness, duelling, and stealing, are forbidden under pain of the severest punishment.

7. If it should be discovered that one of the trades-people has cheated his employer he shall be sentenced not only to make full restitution, but also to pay a third more, as a punishment for his deceitful dealings. Because of this, the Deputies of the Provincial Council shall take care that upon the death of every factor whatever amount he may have had from his employer, which belonged to the employer, shall be assiduously delivered up to him again.

CONCERNING THE LAWS GIVEN BY WILLIAM PENN

Firstly, no one shall be disturbed on account of his belief, but freedom of conscience shall be granted to all inhabitants of the province, so that every nation may build and conduct churches and schools according to their desires.

2. Sunday shall be consecrated to the public worship of God. The teaching of God shall be so zealously carried on that its purity can be recognized in each listener from the fruits which arise from it.

3. For the more convenient bringing up of the youth, the solitary farmers living in the province shall all remove to the market-towns, so that the neighbors may help one another in a Christlike manner and praise God together, and that they may accustom their children also to do the same.

4. The sessions of the court shall be held publicly, at appointed times, so that everyone may attend them.

5. Justices of the peace shall be appointed in the rising cities and market-towns, to insure the observance of the laws.

---

*A Few Selected Laws From William Penn's Laws Concerning his Province by Francis Daniel Pastorius.

6. Cursing, blasphemy, misuse of the name of God, quarrelling, cheating, drunkenness, shall be punished with the pillory.

7. All workmen shall be content with their definite stipulated wages.

8. Each child, that is twelve years of age, shall be put to some handicraft or other honorable trade.

Charter of Georgia 1732

The trustees who founded the colony of Georgia were motivated by humanitarian principles. They planned to establish a colony which would welcome worthy Englishmen who had been reduced to poverty by misfortune. The purpose of the colony is clearly stated in the first part of their charter of Georgia.*

FIFTH YEAR GEORGE II, A. D. 1732

George, the second, by the grace of God, of Great Britain, France, and Ireland, king, defender of the faith, and so forth, to all to whom these presents shall come, greeting:

Whereas we are credibly informed, that many of our poor subjects are, through misfortunes and want of employment, reduced to great necessity, in so much as by their labor they are not able to provide a maintenance for themselves and families; and if they had means to defray their charges and passage, and other expenses incident to new settlements, they would be glad to settle in any of our provinces of America; whereas by cultivating the lands at present waste and desolate, they might not only gain a comfortable subsistence, for themselves and families, but also strengthen our colonies and increase the trade, navigation and wealth of these our realms. And whereas our provinces in North America have been frequently ravaged by Indian enemies, more especially that of South Carolina, which in the late war by the neighboring savages, was laid waste by fire and sword, and great numbers of English inhabitants miserably massacred, and our loving subjects who now inhabit them, by reason of the smallness of their numbers, will, in case of a new war, be exposed to the late calamities, inasmuch as their whole southern frontier continueth unsettled, and lieth open to the savages. And whereas we think it highly becoming our crown and royal dignity, to protect all of our loving subjects, be they ever so distant from us, to extend our fatherly compassion even to the meanest and most infatuated of our people, to relieve the wants of our above mentioned poor subjects; and that it will be highly conducive for accomplishing those ends, that a regular colony of the said poor people be settled and established in the southern territories of Carolina. And whereas we have been well assured, that if we will be graciously pleased to erect and settle a corporation, for the receiving, managing and disposing of the contributions of our loving subjects; divers persons would be induced to contribute to the purposes aforesaid.

* * *

Sinners in the Hands of an Angry God

The following extract is taken from Jonathan Edwards's most famous sermon delivered in 1741 at the height of the Great Awakening, a religious revival which swept the colonies.*

Deuteronomy 32:35.—Their foot shall slide in due time.

In this verse is threatened the vengeance of God on the wicked unbelieving Israelites, that were God's visible people, and lived under means of grace; and that notwithstanding all God's wonderful works that he had wrought towards that people, yet remained, as is expressed verse 28, void of counsel, having no understanding in them; and that, under all the cultivations of heaven, brought forth bitter and poisonous fruit; as in the two verses next preceding the text.

The expression that I have chosen for my text, *their foot shall slide in due time,* seems to imply the following things relating to the punishment and destruction that these wicked Israelites were exposed to:

1. That they were always exposed to destruction; as one that stands or walks in slippery places is always exposed to fall. This is implied in the manner of their destruction's coming upon them, being represented by their foot's sliding. The same is expressed, Psalm 73:18: "Surely thou didst set them in slippery places; thou castedst them down into destruction."

2. It implies that they were always exposed to sudden, unexpected destruction. As he that walks in slippery places is every moment liable to fall, he cannot foresee one moment whether he shall stand or fall the next; and when he does fall, he falls at once,

*The Georgia Charter in Walter McElreath, A TREATISE ON THE CONSTITUTION OF GEORGIA, The Harrison Company, 1912.

*Sinners in the Hands of an Angry God, by Jonathan Edwards in THE WORKS OF JONATHAN EDWARDS, 1843.

without warning, which is also expressed in that Psalm 73:18, 19: "Surely thou didst set them in slippery places; thou castedst them down into destruction: how are they brought into desolation as in a moment."

3. Another thing implied is, that they are liable to fall of themselves, without being thrown down by the hand of another; as he that stands or walks on slippery ground needs nothing but his own weight to throw him down.

4. That the reason why they are not fallen already, and do not fall now, is only that God's appointed time is not come. For it is said that when that due time, or appointed time comes, *their feet shall slide*. Then they shall be left to fall, as they are inclined by their own weight. God will not hold them up in these slippery places any longer, but will let them go; and then, at that very instant, they shall fall into destruction; as he that stands in such slippery declining ground on the edge of a pit that he cannot stand alone, when he is let go he immediately falls and is lost.

The observation from the words that I would now insist upon is this.

There is nothing that keeps wicked men at any one moment out of hell, but the mere pleasure of God.

By the mere pleasure of God, I mean his sovereign pleasure, his arbitrary will, restrained by no obligation, hindered by no manner of difficulty, any more than if nothing else but God's mere will had in the least degree or in any respect whatsoever, any hand in the preservation of wicked men one moment. . . .

* * *

How dreadful is the state of those that are daily and hourly in danger of this great wrath and infinite misery! But this is the dismal case of every soul in this congregation that has not been born again, however moral and strict, sober and religious, they may otherwise be. Oh that you would consider it, whether you be young or old! There is reason to think, that there are many in this congregation now hearing this discourse, that will actually be the subjects of this very misery to all eternity. We know not who they are, or in what seats they sit, or what thoughts they now have. It may be they are now at ease, and hear all these things without much disturbance, and are now flattering themselves that they are not the persons; promising themselves that they shall escape. If we knew that there was one person, and but one, in the whole congregation, that was to be the subject of this misery, what an awful thing it would be to think of! If we knew who it was, what an awful sight would it be to see such a person! How might all the rest of

the congregation lift up a lamentable and bitter cry over him! But alas! Instead of one, how many is it likely will remember this discourse in hell! And it would be a wonder, if some that are now present should not be in hell in a very short time, before this year is out. And it would be no wonder if some persons, that now sit here in some seats of this meeting-house in health, and quiet and secure, should be there before tomorrow morning.

A Cosmopolitan City in the New World

In 1744, Dr. Alexander Hamilton (no relation to the famous Federalist) took a 1600-mile trip through the colonies. The young Scottish-educated physician wrote down his impressions of colonial life, and reprinted here, is his description of Philadelphia.*

Wednesday, June 6, 1744. The country round the city of Philadelphia is level and pleasant. . . . The city lies betwixt the . . . Delaware and Skuylkill, the streets being laid out in rectangular squares which makes a regular, uniform plan, but . . . altogether destitute of variety.

At my entering the city, I observed the regularity of the streets, but at the same time the majority of the houses are mean and low and much decayed, the streets in general not paved, very dirty, and obstructed with rubbish and lumber (for new construction). The State House, Assembly House (now known as Independence Hall), the great church in Second Street, and Whitefield church are good buildings.

I observed several comical, grotesque faces in the inn where I put up which would have afforded a variety of hints for a painter like Hogarth. (An English artist whose caricatures were as popular in America as they were in England.) They talked at the inn upon all subjects—politics, religion, and trade—some tolerably well, but most of them ignorantly. . . .

I was shaved by a little . . . old barber who kept dancing round me and talking all the time . . . and yet did his job lightly and to a hair. He abounded in compliments and was a very civil fellow in his way. He told me he had been a journeyman for 40 . . . years, notwithstanding which, he understood how to trim gentlemen as well . . . as the best masters. . . .

Thursday, June 7. I saw one instance of industry

*Carl Bridenbaugh (ed.), GENTLEMAN'S PROGRESS: THE ITINERARIUM OF DR. ALEXANDER HAMILTON, published for the Institute of Early American History and Culture by the University of North Carolina Press, 1948. As it appears in Richard C. Brown, THE HUMAN SIDE OF HISTORY, Ginn & Co. Reprinted by permission.

as soon as I got up and looked out ... my chamber window, and that was the shops open at 5 in the morning. . . .

Friday, June 8. . . . I dined at a tavern with a very mixed company of different nations and religions. There were Scots, English, Dutch, Germans, and Irish; there were Roman Catholics, Church (of England) men, Presbyterians, Quakers, Newlightmen, Methodists, Seventh day men, Moravians, Anabaptists, and one Jew. The whole company consisted of 25 planted around an oblong table in a great hall well supplied with flies. . . . The prevailing topic of conversation was politics and conjectures of a French war (King George's War in which the colonies became involved in 1744). A knot of Quakers . . . talked only about selling of flour and the low price it bore. The whole company touched a little upon religion, and high words arose among some . . . but their blood was not hot enough to quarrel. . . .

In the afternoon I went to see some ships that lay in the river. Among the rest were three vessels a fitting out for privateers. . . . At six o'clock I went to the coffee house and drank a dish of coffee. . . .

Saturday, June 9th. This morning there fell a light rain which proved very refreshing, the weather having been very hot and dry for several days. The heat in this city is excessive, the sun's rays being reflected with such power from the brick houses and from the street pavement which is brick. The people commonly use awnings of painted cloth or canvas over their shop windows and doors and, at sun set, throw buckets full of water upon the pavement which cools it. They have plenty of excellent water in this city, there being a pump at almost every 50 paces distance. There are a great number of balconies to their houses where sometimes the men sit in cool clothes and smoke.

The market in this city is perhaps the largest in North America. It is kept twice a week upon Wednesdays and Saturdays. The street where it stands, called Market Street, is large and spacious, composed of the best houses in the city.

They have but one public clock here which strikes the hour but has neither index nor dial plate. It is strange they should lack such an ornament and convenience in so large a city but the chief part of the community consisting of Quakers, they would seem to shun ornament in their public buildings as well as in their clothing. . . .

Here is no public magazine of arms nor any method of defense . . . in case of the invasion of an enemy. This is owing to the obstinacy of the Quakers in maintaining their principle of non-resistance. . . .

Tuesday, June 12. In Philadelphia one may live tolerably cheap as to articles of eating and drinking, but European goods here are extravagantly dear. Even goods of their own manufacture such as linen, woolen, and leather bear a high price. . . .

Wednesday, June 13. Early in the morning I left Philadelphia, being willing to depart that city where, because of the excessive heat, it was a pain to live and breath. . . .

Music and History

The sources of history are more than inaugural addresses of presidents and the legal language of congressional acts. They are also the words, the customs, and the thoughts of ordinary people. Popular music and songs often reflect the mood of the times better than do mere documents.

Folk ballads and popular songs have expressed the feelings and attitudes of Americans in all periods of their history. Colonial Americans brought their music with them from their homelands in Europe, Africa, and Asia. Native singers later began to supply new words, rhythms, and melodies more suitable to the American setting.

Colonists sang "Yankee Doodle" in the 1770s during the Revolutionary War, expressing defiance of Great Britain and mocking British "macaronies" (London dandies who wore extreme fashions). Negro slaves expressed their sorrow in songs such as "Nobody Knows the Trouble I've Seen." Their hope of freedom was expressed in "Go Down Moses."

Americans made songs about their adventures as they moved westward to settle, songs about the canals they dug and the railroads they built. Hard times and good times can be seen in the songs Americans sang. There were hymns, songs for work and play, songs and ballads about events that captured the public imagination.

Wars often were the inspiration for songs of patriotism or songs expressing dedication to a great cause. "The Star Spangled Banner" was written during the War of 1812 on the morning after the bombardment of Fort McHenry. "The Battle Hymn of the Republic" expressed the deeply religious spirit of those who saw the Civil War as a great crusade against slavery. World War I brought songs of protest—"I Didn't Raise My Boy to Be a Soldier"—and answers to those protests—"America, Here's My Boy." Sentiment against Americans of foreign birth ran high and was expressed in songs such as "Don't Bite the Hand That's Feeding You."

Changing social patterns and national attitudes were also reflected in popular music. The movement of population from rural to urban areas, and the employment of more and more women in business were reflected in the titles and words to songs such as "In the Heart of the City That Has No Heart" and "Heaven Will Protect the Working Girl." The advent of the automobile was celebrated in "In My Merry Oldsmobile" and the great exposition of 1904 adopted for its theme an invitation to "Meet Me in St. Louis." The extreme nationalism and imperialism of the era of Theodore Roosevelt were expressed in music. (The word "Jingoism," meaning extreme nationalism, was borrowed from a popular song.) Flappers of the 1920s showed their defiance of conventions by wearing short skirts with stockings rolled below the knee. They sang a song urging young women to "roll 'em girls, roll 'em, roll 'em and show your pretty knees."

The end of Prohibition and the beginning of the Roosevelt administration offered a moment of optimism during the Great Depression. People sang and danced to "Happy Days Are Here Again." The hard times of the 1930s were described in songs about unemployment—"Brother Can You Spare a Dime"—or the misery of those who could find only the most degrading kinds of work—"Ten Cents a Dance." Union members sang "We Shall Overcome," and later (with additional words) the song was the theme of Negroes seeking civil liberties and equal rights.

Young people found their own music, which was often shocking to or not understood by their elders. It was often music for dancing. Ragtime was the music of the young before 1920. The 1920s became the "jazz age." "Swing" prevailed during the 1930s and 1940s. By the 1950s the music of the younger generation had begun to reflect a new interest in folk ballads and the sounds and rhythms of "rock." This continued into the 1960s with the addition of songs of protest—against war, "Where Have All the Flowers Gone"—against discrimination, "We Shall Overcome"—against conformity, "Little Boxes." Others told of isolation, "The Sound of Silence"—of a need for love, "What the World Needs Now Is Love"—and of disillusion with the past and hope for the future, "Aquarius" and "Let the Sunshine In."

There are many excellent collections of American folk songs, ballads, and popular music. They help to tell a part of the story of America and its people that cannot be found in conventional books of history. A few books about American music are *Panorama of American Popular Music* and *American Popular Songs from the Revolutionary War to the Present* by David Ewen; *Grace Notes on American History: Popular Sheet Music from 1820-1900* by Lester S. Levy; *Folk Song: U.S.A.* by John and Alan Lomax; *The Ballad of America: A History of the United States in Song and Story* by John Anthony Scott; and *History of Popular Music* by Sigmund Spaeth.

There are excellent collections of American music in libraries and museums in all parts of the country. Some outstanding collections are to be found in the Library of Congress and in the National Archives in Washington, D.C.

"Young Ladies in Town"

After the French and Indian War, Great Britain wanted to keep colonists from the lands that had been won from France. Britain also wanted to collect taxes from the colonies to help pay for the cost of the war against France. When the Townshend Acts of 1767 were passed, American colonists boycotted British manufactures rather than pay duties on imports. This song appeared in the *Boston Newsletter* in 1769. Urging young ladies to wear only clothes of American manufacture, it encouraged them to refuse to have anything to do with those men who wore fine clothes imported from England. ("Bohea" was a kind of black tea imported from China; "hyson" was a kind of green Chinese tea.)*

Young la-dies in town, and those that live round, Wear none but your own coun-try lin-en; Of e-con-o-my boast, let your pride be the most To show clothes of your own make and spin-ning. What if home-spun, they say. be not quite so gay As bro-cades, be not in a pas-sion; For once it is known, 'tis much worn in town, One and all will cry out, 'tis the fash-ion!

And as one all agree that you'll not married be
  To such as will wear London factory;
But at first sight refuse, tell 'em you will choose
  As encourage our own manufactory.
No more ribbons wear, nor in rich silks appear,
  Love your country much better than fine things;
Begin without passion, 'twill soon be the fashion
  To grace your smooth locks with a twine string.

Throw away your bohea, and your green hyson tea
  And all things of a new-fashioned duty;
Get in a good store of the choice Labrador
  There'll soon be enough here to suit ye.
These do without fear, and to all you'll appear
  Fair, charming, true, lovely, and clever;
Though the times remain darkish, young men will be sparkish,
  And love you much stronger than ever.

*From THE BALLAD OF AMERICA: THE HISTORY OF THE UNITED STATES IN SONG AND STORY by John Anthony Scott. Copyright © 1966 by Bantam Books, Inc.

The Fall of Quebec

The best-known battle of the French and Indian War was fought on the Plains of Abraham just outside of the city of Quebec, in September 1759. As related in the following eyewitness account, both generals, James Wolfe of Britain and Marquis de Montcalm of France, died as a result of battle wounds. The British forces had to scale "one of the steepest precipices that can be conceived, being almost a perpendicular, and of an incredible height," in order to attack Quebec. The British victory here and later at Montreal ended French control in North America.*

... Great preparations are making, throughout the fleet and army, to surprise the enemy, and compel them to decide the fate of Quebec by a battle: all the long-boats below the town are to be filled with seamen, marines, and such detachments as can be spared from Points Levi and Orleans, in order to make a feint off Beauport and the Point de Lest, and endeavour to engross the attention of the Sieur de Montcalm, while the army are to force a descent on this side of the town. The Officer of our regiment, who commanded the escort yesterday on the reconnoitring party, being asked, in the General's hearing, after the health of one of the gentlemen who was reported to be ill, replied,—'he was in a very low indifferent state;' which the other lamented, saying, 'he has but a puny, delicate constitution.'—This struck his Excellency, it being his own case, who interrupted, 'Don't tell me of constitution, that Officer has good spirits, and good spirits will carry a man through every thing.' ...

The Brigadiers Monckton and Murray, with the troops under their command, reimbarked this day, from the parish of St. Nicholas, and returned to their ships. This evening all the boats of the fleet below the town were filled with marines, &c. &c. covered by frigates and sloops of war, worked up, and lay half-channel over, opposite to Beauport, as if intending to land in the morning, and thereby fix the enemy's whole attention to that quarter; the ships attending them are to edge over, at break of day, as near as possible without grounding, and cannonade the French intrenchments. At nine o'clock this night, our army in high spirits, the first division of them put into the flat-bottomed boats, and, in a short time after, the whole squadron moved up the river with the tide of flood, and, about an hour before day-light

next morning, we fell down with the ebb. Weather favourable, a star-light night.

Thursday, September 13, 1759.

Before day-break this morning we made a descent upon the north shore, about half a quarter of a mile to the eastward of Sillery; and the light troops were fortunately, by the rapidity of the current, carried lower down, between us and Cape Diamond; we had, in this debarkation, thirty flat-bottomed boats, containing about sixteen hundred men. This was a great surprise on the enemy, who, from the natural strength of the place, did not suspect, and consequently were not prepared against, so bold an attempt. The chain of centries, which they had posted along the summit of the heights, galled us a little, and picked off several men, and some Officers, before our light infantry got up to dislodge them. This grand enterprise was conducted, and executed with great good order and discretion; as fast as we landed, the boats put off for reinforcements, and the troops formed with much regularity: the General, with Brigadiers Monckton and Murray, were a-shore with the first division. We lost no time here, but clambered up one of the steepest precipices that can be conceived, being almost a perpendicular, and of an incredible height. As soon as we gained the summit, all was quiet, and not a shot was heard, owing to the excellent conduct of the light infantry under Colonel Howe; it was by this time clear day-light. Here we formed again, the river and the south country in our rear, our right extending to the town, our left to Sillery, and halted a few minutes. The General then detached the light troops to our left to route the enemy from their battery, and to disable their guns, except they could be rendered serviceable to the party who were to remain there; and this service was soon performed. We then faced to the right, and marched towards the town by files, till we came to the plains of Abraham; an even piece of ground which Mr. Wolfe had made choice of, while we stood forming upon the hill. Weather showery: about six o'clock the enemy first made their appearance upon the heights, between us and the town; whereupon we halted, and wheeled to the right, thereby forming the line of battle. ... The enemy had now likewise formed the line of battle, and got some cannon to play on us, with round and canister-shot; but what galled us most was a body of Indians and other marksmen they had concealed in the corn opposite to the front of our right wing, and a coppice that stood opposite to our center, inclining towards our left; but the Colonel Hale, by Brigadier Monckton's orders, advanced some platoons, alternately, from the forty-seventh regi-

---

*Eyewitness Account of the Fall of Quebec by John Knox.

ment, which, after a few rounds, obliged these sculkers to retire: we were now ordered to lie down, and remained some time in this position. About eight o'clock we had two pieces of short brass six-pounders playing on the enemy, which threw them into some confusion, and obliged them to alter their disposition, and Montcalm formed them into three large columns; about nine the two armies moved a little nearer each other. The light cavalry made a faint attempt upon our parties at the battery of Sillery, but were soon beat off, and Monsieur de Bougainville, with his troops from Cape Rouge, came down to attack the flank of our second line, hoping to penetrate there; but, by a masterly disposition of Brigadier Townshend, they were forced to desist, and the third battalion of Royal Americans was then detached to the first ground we had formed on after we gained the heights, to preserve the communication with the beach and our boats. About ten o'clock the enemy began to advance briskly in three columns, with loud shouts and recovered arms, two of them inclining to the left of our army, and the third towards our right, firing obliquely at the two extremities of our line, from the distance of one hundred and thirty—, until they came within forty yards; which our troops withstood with the greatest intrepidity and firmness, still reserving their fire, and paying the strictest obedience to their Officers: this uncommon steadiness, together with the havoc which the grape-shot from our fieldpieces made among them, threw them into some disorder, and was most critically maintained by a well-timed, regular, and heavy discharge of our small arms, such as they could no longer oppose; hereupon they gave way, and fled with precipitation, so that, by the time the cloud of smoke was vanished, our men were again loaded, and, profiting by the advantage we had over them, pursued them almost to the gates of the town, and the bridge over the little river, redoubling our fire with great eagerness, making many Officers and men prisoners. The weather cleared up, with a comfortably warm sun-shine: the Highlanders chaced them vigorously towards Charles's river, and the fifty-eighth to the suburb close to John's gate, until they were checked by the cannon from the two hulks; at the same time a gun, which the town had brought to bear upon us with grapeshot, galled the progress of the regiments to the right, who were likewise pursuing with equal ardour, while Colonel Hunt Walsh, by a very judicious movement, wheeled the battalions of Bragg and Kennedy to the left, and flanked the coppice where a body of the enemy made a stand, as if willing to renew the action; but a few platoons from these corps completed our victory. Then it was that Brigadier Townshend came

up, called off the pursuers, ordered the whole line to dress, and recover their former ground. Our joy at this success is inexpressibly damped by the loss we sustained of one of the greatest heroes which this or any other age can boast of,—GENERAL JAMES WOLFE, who received his mortal wound, as he was exerting himself at the head of the grenadiers of Louisbourg. . . .

. . . The Sieur de Montcalm died late last night; when his wound was dressed, and he settled in bed, the Surgeons who attended him were desired to acquaint him ingenuously with their sentiments of him, and, being answered that his wound was mortal, he calmly replied, 'he was glad of it': his Excellency then demanded,—'whether he could survive it long, and how long?' He was told, 'about a dozen hours, perhaps more, peradventure less.' 'So much the better,' rejoined this eminent warrior; 'I am happy I shall not live to see the surrender of Quebec.' . . .

After our late worthy General, of renowned memory, was carried off wounded, to the rear of the front line, he desired those who were about him to lay him down; being asked if he would have a Surgeon? he replied, 'it is needless; it is all over with me.' One of them then cried out, 'they run, see how they run.' 'Who runs!' demanded our hero, with great earnestness, like a person roused from sleep? The Officer answered, 'The enemy, Sir; Egad they give way every-where.' Thereupon the General rejoined, *'Go one of you, my lads, to Colonel Burton—; tell him to march Webb's regiment with all speed down to Charles's river, to cut off the retreat of the fugitives from the bridge.'* Then, turning on his side, he added, *'Now, God be praised, I will die in peace:'* and thus expired.

Benjamin Franklin Opposes the Stamp Act

No event gave Benjamin Franklin as much publicity in Europe as did his examination before the British House of Commons, February 1766, concerning the repeal of the Stamp Act. His testimony describing American views of taxation, Parliament, commerce, and American self-sufficiency, was translated into French and widely circulated in Europe.*

---

*The Testimony of Benjamin Franklin in the British House of Commons Concerning the Repeal of the American Stamp Act.

Q. What is your name, and place of abode?

A. Franklin, of Philadelphia.

Q. Do the Americans pay any considerable taxes among themselves?

A. Certainly many, and very heavy taxes.

Q. What are the present taxes in Pennsylvania, laid by the laws of the colony?

A. There are taxes on all estates real and personal, a poll tax, a tax on all offices, professions, trades and businesses, according to their profits; an excise on all wine, rum, and other spirits; and a duty of Ten Pounds per head on all Negroes imported, with some other duties.

Q. For what purposes are those taxes laid?

A. For the support of the civil and military establishments of the country, and to discharge the heavy debt contracted in the last war.

Q. Are not all the people very able to pay those taxes?

A. No. The frontier counties, all along the continent, having been frequently ravaged by the enemy and greatly impoverished, are able to pay very little tax. And therefore, in consideration of their distresses, our late tax laws do expressly favour those counties, excusing the sufferers; and I suppose the same is done in other governments.

Q. Are not you concerned in the management of the Post-Office in America?

A. Yes. I am Deputy Post-Master General of North-America.

Q. Don't you think the distribution of stamps by post to all the inhabitants very practicable, if there was no opposition?

A. The posts only go along the seacoasts; they do not, except in a few instances, go back into the country; and if they did, sending for stamps by post would occasion an expence of postage amounting, in many cases, to much more than that of the stamps themselves.

Q. From the thinness of the back settlements, would not the stamp act be extremely inconvenient to the inhabitants, if executed?

A. To be sure it would; as many of the inhabitants could not get stamps when they had occasion for them without taking long journeys, and spending perhaps Three or Four Pounds, that the Crown might get Six pence.

Q. Are not the Colonies, from their circumstances, very able to pay the stamp duty?

A. In my opinion there is not gold and silver enough in the Colonies to pay the stamp duty for one year.

Q. Don't you know that the money arising from the stamps was all to be laid out in America?

A. I know it is appropriated by the act to the American service; but it will be spent in the conquered Colonies, where the soldiers are, not in the Colonies that pay it.

Q. Is there not a balance of trade due from the Colonies where the troops are posted, that will bring back the money to the old colonies?

A. I think not. I believe very little would come back. I know of no trade likely to bring it back. I think it would come from the Colonies where it was spent directly to England; for I have always observed, that in every Colony the more plenty the means of remittance to England, the more goods are sent for, and the more trade with England carried on.

Q. Do you think it right that America should be protected by this country and pay no part of the expence?

A. That is not the case. The Colonies raised, cloathed and payed, during the last war, near 25000 men, and spent many millions.

Q. Were you not reimbursed by parliament?

A. We were only reimbursed what, in your opinion, we had advanced beyond our proportion, or beyond what might reasonably be expected from us; and it was a very small part of what we spent. Pennsylvania, in particular, disbursed about 500,000 Pounds, and the reimbursements, in the whole, did not exceed 60,000 Pounds.

Q. Do not you think the people of America would submit to pay the stamp duty, if it was moderated?

A. No, never, unless compelled by force of arms.

Q. What was the temper of America towards Great Britain before the year 1763?

A. The best in the world. They submitted willingly to the government of the Crown, and paid, in all their courts, obedience to acts of parliament. Numerous as the people are in the several provinces, they cost you nothing in forts, citadels, garrisons, or armies, to keep them in subjection. They were governed by this country at the expence only of a little pen, ink and paper. They were led by a thread. They had not only a respect, but an affection for Great-Britain; for its laws, its customs and manners, and even a fondness for its fashions, that greatly increased the commerce. Natives of Britain were always treated with particular regard; to be an Old-England man was, of itself, a character of some respect, and gave a kind of rank among us.

Q. And what is their temper now?

A. O, very much altered.

Q. Did you ever hear the authority of parliament to make laws for America questioned till lately?

A. The authority of parliament was allowed to be

valid in all laws, except such as should lay internal taxes. It was never disputed in laying duties to regulate commerce.

Q. In what light did the people of America use to consider the parliament of Great-Britain?

A. They considered the parliament as the great bulwark and security of their liberties and privileges, and always spoke of it with the utmost respect and veneration. Arbitrary ministers, they thought, might possibly, at times, attempt to oppress them; but they relied on it, that the parliament, on application, would always give redress. They remembered, with gratitude, a strong instance of this, when a bill was brought into parliament, with a clause, to make royal instructions laws in the colonies, which the House of Commons would not pass, and it was thrown out.

Q. And have they not still the same respect for parliament?

A. No, it is greatly lessened.

Q. To what causes is that owing?

A. To a concurrence of causes; the restraints lately laid on their trade, by which the bringing of foreign gold and silver into the Colonies was prevented; the prohibition of making paper money among themselves; and then demanding a new and heavy tax by stamps; taking away, at the same time, trials by juries, and refusing to receive and hear their humble petitions.

Q. Don't you think they would submit to the stamp-act, if it was modified, the obnoxious parts taken out, and the duty reduced to some particulars, of small moment?

A. No; they will never submit to it.

Q. What do you think is the reason that the people of America increase faster than in England?

A. Because they marry younger, and more generally.

Q. Why so?

A. Because any young couple, that are industrious, may easily obtain land of their own, on which they can raise a family.

Q. Are not the lower rank of people more at their ease in America than in England?

A. They may be so, if they are sober and diligent, as they are better paid for their labour.

Q. What is your opinion of a future tax, imposed on the same principle with that of the stamp-act? How would the Americans receive it?

A. Just as they do this. They would not pay it.

Q. Have not you heard of the resolutions of this House, and of the House of Lords, asserting the right of parliament relating to America, including a power to tax the people there?

A. Yes, I have heard of such resolutions.

Q. What will be the opinion of the Americans on those resolutions?

A. They will think them unconstitutional and unjust.

Q. Was it an opinion in America before 1763, that the parliament had no right to lay taxes and duties there?

A. I never heard any objection to the right of laying duties to regulate commerce; but a right to lay internal taxes was never supposed to be in parliament, as we are not represented there.

Q. On what do you found your opinion, that the people in America made any such distinction?

A. I know that whenever the subject has occurred in conversation where I have been present, it has appeared to be the opinion of every one, that we could not be taxed by a parliament where we were not represented.

Q. You say the Colonies have always submitted to external taxes, and object to the right of parliament only in laying internal taxes; now can you shew, that there is any kind of difference between the two taxes to the Colony on which they may be laid?

A. I think the difference is very great. An external tax is a duty laid on commodities imported; that duty is added to the first cost and other charges on the commodity, and, when it is offered to sale, makes a part of the price. If the people do not like it at that price, they refuse it; they are not obliged to pay it. But an internal tax is forced from the people without their consent, if not laid by their own representatives. The stamp act says, we shall have no commerce, make no exchange of property with each other, neither purchase, nor grant, nor recover debts; we shall neither marry nor make our wills, unless we pay such and such sums; and thus it is intended to extort our money from us, or ruin us by the consequences of refusing to pay it.

Q. But supposing the internal tax or duty to be laid on the necessaries of life, imported into your colony, will not that be the same thing in its effects as an internal tax?

A. I do not know a single article imported into the Northern Colonies, but what they can either do without, or make themselves.

Q. Considering the resolutions of parliament, as to the right, do you think, if the stamp act is repealed, that the North Americans will be satisfied?

A. I believe they will.

Q. Why do you think so?

A. I think the resolutions of right will give them very little concern, if they are never attempted to be carried into practice. The Colonies will probably consider themselves in the same situation, in that respect, with Ireland; they know you claim the same right with regard to Ireland, but you never exercise it. And they may believe you never will exercise it in the Colonies, any more than in Ireland, unless on some very extraordinary occasion.

Q. But who are to be the judges of that extraordinary occasion? Is not the parliament?

A. Though the parliament may judge of the occasion, the people will think it can never exercise such right, till representatives from the Colonies are admitted into parliament; and that, when ever the occasion arises, representatives will be ordered.

Q. Did the Americans ever dispute the controuling power of parliament to regulate the commerce?

A. No.

Q. Can any thing less than a military force carry the stamp act into execution?

A. I do not see how a military force can be applied to that purpose.

Q. Why may it not?

A. Suppose a military force sent into America, they will find nobody in arms; what are they then to do? They cannot force a man to take stamps who chuses to do without them. They will not find a rebellion; they may indeed make one.

Q. If the act is not repealed, what do you think will be the consequences?

A. A total loss of the respect and affection the people of America bear to this country, and of all the commerce that depends on that respect and affection.

Q. If the stamp act should be repealed, would not the Americans think they could oblige the parliament to repeal every external tax-law now in force?

A. It is hard to answer questions of what people at such a distance will think.

Q. But what do you imagine they will think were the motives of repealing the act?

A. I suppose they will think it was repealed from a conviction of its inexpediency; and they will reply upon it, that while the same inexpediency subsists, you will never attempt to make such another.

Q. What do you mean by its inexpediency?

A. I mean its inexpediency on several accounts; the poverty and inability of those who were to pay the tax; the general discontent it has occasioned; and the impracticability of enforcing it.

Q. If the act should be repealed, and the legislature should shew its resentment to the opposers of the stamp act, would the Colonies acquiesce in the authority of the legislture? What is your opinion they would do?

A. I don't doubt at all, that if the legislature repeal the stamp act, the Colonies will acquiesce in the authority.

Q. Is it not necessary to send troops to America, to defend the Americans against the Indians?

A. No, by no means; it never was necessary. They defended themselves when they were but a handful, and the Indians much more numerous. They continually gained ground, and have driven the Indians over the mountains, without any troops sent to their assistance from this country. And can it be thought necessary now to send troops for their defence from those diminished Indian tribes, when the Colonies are become so populous and so strong? There is not the least occasion for it; they are very able to defend themselves.

Q. If the stamp act should be repealed, would it induce the assemblies of America to acknowledge the rights of parliament to tax them, and would they erase their resolutions?

A. No, never.

Q. Are there no means of obliging them to erase those resolutions?

A. None that I know of; they will never do it, unless compelled by force of arms.

Q. Is there a power on earth that can force them to erase them?

A. No power, how great soever, can force men to change their opinions.

Q. What used to be the pride of the Americans?

A. To indulge in the fashions and manufactures of Great Britain.

Q. What is now their pride?

A. To wear their old cloaths over again, till they can make new ones.

William Pitt's Speech Against American Taxation

William Pitt, later Lord Chatham, was an outstanding leader of Britain during most of the Seven Years' War (1756-1763). In a speech before the House of Commons in 1766, Pitt challenged his colleagues to reconsider their taxation of the American colonies. He raised the issue of taxation without actual representation and evaluated the difference between external and internal taxation. Pitt demanded "that the Stamp Act be repealed absolutely, totally, and immediately" because "Americans have been wronged."

Gentlemen, Sir (to the Speaker), I have been charged with giving birth to sedition in America.

They have spoken their sentiments with freedom against this unhappy act, and that freedom has become their crime. Sorry I am to hear the liberty of speech in this House imputed as a crime. But the imputation shall not discourage me. It is a liberty I mean to exercise. No gentleman ought to be afraid to exercise it. It is a liberty by which the gentleman who calumniates it might have profited. He ought to have desisted from his project. The gentleman tells us, America is obstinate; America is almost in open rebellion. I rejoice that America has resisted. Three millions of people so dead to all the feelings of liberty, as voluntarily to submit to be slaves, would have been fit instruments to make slaves of the rest. I come not here armed at all points, with law cases and acts of Parliament, with the statute-book doubled down in dog's-ears, to defend the cause of liberty: if I had, I myself would have cited the two cases of Chester and Durham. I would have cited them, to have shewn that, even under former arbitrary reigns, Parliaments were ashamed of taxing a people without their consent, and allowed them representatives. . . . The gentleman tells us of many who are taxed, and are not represented.—The India Company, merchants, stockholders, manufacturers. Surely many of these are represented in other capacities, as owners of land, or as freemen of boroughs. It is a misfortune that more are not equally represented. But they are all inhabitants, and as such, are they not virtually represented? Many have it in their option to be actually represented. They have connections with those that elect, and they have influence over them. . . .

. . . The gentleman boasts of his bounties to America! Are not these bounties intended finally for the benefit of this kingdom? If they are not, he has misapplied the national treasures. I am no courtier of America—I stand up for this kingdom. I maintain, that the Parliament has a right to bind, to restrain America. Our legislative power over the colonies is sovereign and supreme. When it ceases to be sovereign and supreme, I would advise every gentleman to sell his lands, if he can, and embark for that country. When two countries are connected together, like England and her colonies, without being incorporated, the one must necessarily govern; the greater must rule the less; but so rule it, as not to contradict the fundamental principles that are common to both.

If the gentleman does not understand the difference between external and internal taxes, I cannot help it; but there is a plain distinction between taxes levied for the purposes of raising a revenue, and duties imposed for the regulation of trade, for the accommodation of the subject; although, in the con-

sequences, some revenue might incidentally arise from the latter.

The gentleman asks, when were the colonies emancipated? But I desire to know, when they were made slaves? But I dwell not upon words. When I had the honour of serving his Majesty, I availed myself of the means of information, which I derived from my office: I speak, therefore from knowledge. My materials were good, I was at pains to collect, to digest, to consider them; and I will be bold to affirm, that the profits to Great Britain from the trade of the colonies, through all its branches, is two millions a year. This is the fund that carried you triumphantly through the last war. The estates that were rented at two thousand pounds a year, threescore years ago, are at three thousand pounds at present. Those estates sold then from fifteen to eighteen years purchase; the same may now be sold for thirty. You owe this to America. This is the price America pays for her protection. And shall a miserable financier come with a boast, that he can bring a pepper-corn into the Exchequer, to the loss of millions to the nation! I dare not say, how much higher these profits may be augmented. Omitting the immense increase of people by natural population, in the northern colonies, and the emigration from every part of Europe, I am convinced the commercial system of America may be altered to advantage. You have prohibited where you ought to have encouraged, and encouraged where you ought to have prohibited. . . .

A great deal has been said without doors, of the power, of the strength of America. It is a topic that ought to be cautiously meddled with. In a good cause, on a sound bottom, the force of this country can crush America to atoms. I know the valour of your troops. I know the skill of your officers. There is not a company of foot that has served in America, out of which you may not pick a man of sufficient knowledge and experience to make a governor of a colony there. But on this ground, on the Stamp Act, when so many here will think it a crying injustice, I am one who will lift up my hands against it.

In such a cause, your success would be hazardous. America, if she fell, would fall like the strong man. She would embrace the pillars of the state, and pull down the constitution along with her. Is this your boasted peace? Not to sheath the sword in its scabbard, but to sheath it in the bowels of your countrymen? Will you quarrel with yourselves; now the whole House of Bourbon is united against you? . . . . The Americans have not acted in all things with prudence and temper. The Americans have been wronged. They have been driven to madness by injustice. Will you punish them for the madness you have occasioned? Rather let prudence and temper come first from this side. I will undertake for America, that she will follow the example. There are two lines in a ballad of *Prior's,* of a man's behaviour to his wife, so applicable to you, and your colonies, that I cannot help repeating them:

> *Be to her faults a little blind:*
> *Be to her virtues very kind.*

Upon the whole, I will beg leave to tell the House what is really my opinion. It is, that the Stamp Act be *repealed absolutely, totally,* and *immediately.* That the reason for the repeal be assigned, because it was founded on an erroneous principle. At the same time, let the sovereign authority of this country over the colonies be asserted in as strong terms as can be devised, and be made to extend to every point of legislation whatsoever. That we may bind their *trade,* confine their *manufactures,* and exercise every *power* whatsoever, except that of taking their money out of their pockets without their consent.

The Boston Massacre

A Boston merchant, John Tudor, was an eyewitness to the Boston Massacre, March 5, 1770. Four Bostonians died when British soldiers opened fire on a group of civilians who had been throwing snowballs at them. John Adams defended the soldiers at their trial which resulted in the acquittal of all except two, who were branded on the hand.*

On Monday Evening the 5th current, a few Minutes after 9 O'Clock a most horrid murder was committed in King Street before the Customhouse Door by 8 or 9 Soldiers under the Command of Capt Thos Preston drawn of from the Main Guard on the South side of the Townhouse.

This unhappy affair began by Some Boys & young fellows throwing Snow Balls at the sentry placed at the Customhouse Door. On which 8 or 9 Soldiers Came to his assistance. Soon after a Number of people colected, when the Capt commanded the Soldiers to fire, which they did and 3 Men were Kil'd on the Spot & several Mortaly Wounded, one of which died next morning. The Capt soon drew off his Soldiers up to the Main Guard, or the Consequencis mite have been terable, for on the Guns fiering the people

were alarmd & set the Bells a Ringing as if for Fire, which drew Multitudes to the place of action. Levt Governor Hutchinson, who was commander in Chefe, was sent for & Came to the Council Chamber, w[h]ere som of the Magistrates attended. The Governor desired the Multitude about 10 O'Clock to sepperat & go home peaceable & he would do all in his power that Justice shold be don &c. The 29 Rigiment being then under Arms on the south side of the Townhouse, but the people insisted that the Soldiers should be ordered to their Barracks 1st before they would sepperat, Which being don the people sepperated aboute 1 O'Clock.—Capt Preston was taken up by a warrent given to the high Sherif by Justice Dania & Tudor and came under Examination about 2 O'Clock & we sent him to Goal soon after 3, having Evidence sufficient, to committ him, on his ordering the soldiers to fire: So aboute 4 O'Clock the Town became quiet. The next forenoon the 8 Soldiers that fired on the inhabitants was allso sent to Goal. Tuesday A.M. the inhabitants mett at Faneuil Hall & after som pertinant speches, chose a Committee of 15 Gentlemn to waite on the Levt. Governor in Council to request the immediate removeal of the Troops. The message was in these Words. That it is the unanimous opinion of this Meeting, that the inhabitants & soldiery can no longer live together in safety; that nothing can Ratonaly be expected to restore the peace of the Town & prevent Blood & Carnage, but the removal of the Troops: and that we most fervently pray his Honor that his power & influance may be exerted for their instant removal. His Honor's Reply was. Gentlmen I am extreemly sorry for the unhappy difference & especially of the last Evening & Signifieng that it was not in his power to remove the Troops &c &c.

The Above Reply was not satisfactory to the Inhabitants, as but one Rigiment should be removed to the Castle Barracks. In the afternoon the Town Adjourned to Dr Sewill's Meetinghouse, for Fanieul Hall was not larg enough to hold the people, their being at least 3,000, som supos'd near 4,000, when they chose a Committee to waite on the Levt. Governor to let him & the Council Know that nothing less will satisfy the people, then a total & immediate removal of the Troops oute of the Town.—His Honor laid before the Council the Vote of the Town. The Council thereon expressed themselves to be unanimously of opinion that it was absolutely Necessary for his Majesty service, the good order of the Town &c that the Troops Should be immidtly removed oute of the Town.—His Honor communicated this advice of the Council to Col Dalrymple & desir'd he would order the Troops down to Castle William.

Eyewitness Account of the Boston Massacre, by John Tudor.

After the Col. had seen the Vote of the Council He gave his Word & honor to the Town's Committee that both the Rigiments should be remov'd without delay. The Com^te return'd to the Town Meeting & Mr Hancock, chairman of the Com^te Read their Report as above, which was Received with a shoute & clap of hands, which made the Meetinghouse Ring: So the Meeting was dessolved and a great number of Gentlemen appear'd to Watch the Center of the Town & the prison, which continued for 11 Nights and all was quiet again, as the Soldiers was all moved of to the Castle.

(Thursday) Agreeable to a general request of the Inhabitants, were follow'd to the Grave (for they were all Buried in one) in succession the 4 Bodies of Mess^s Saml Gray Saml Maverick James Caldwell & Crispus Attucks, the unhappy Victims who fell in the Bloody Massacre. On this sorrowfull Occasion most of the shops & stores in Town were shut, all the Bells were order'd to toll a solom peal in Boston, Charleston, Cambridge & Roxbery. The several Hearses forming a junction in King Street, the Theatre of that inhuman Tradgedy, proceeded from thence thro' the main street, lengthened by an immence Concourse of people, So numerous as to be obliged to follow in Ranks of 4 & 6 abreast and brought up by a long Train of Carriages. The sorrow Visible in the Countenances, together with the peculiar solemnity, Surpass description, it was suppos'd that the Spectators & those that follow'd the corps amounted to 15000, som supposed 20,000. Note Capt Preston was tried for his Life on the affare of the above Octob^r 24 1770. The Trial lasted 5 Days, but the Jury brought him in not Guilty.

Slaves Petition for Freedom

The desire for liberty that grew in the colonies before the Revolutionary War was not limited to white colonists. Negro slaves of Massachusetts submitted the following petition for their freedom in 1773, setting forth the idea that freedom was a natural right of man, much as the Declaration of Independence would do a few years later.*

Boston, April 20th, 1773

Sir, the efforts made by the legislative of this province in their last sessions to free themselves from slavery, gave us, who are in that deplorable state, a

*From Herbert Aptheker, A DOCUMENTARY HISTORY OF THE NEGRO PEOPLE IN THE UNITED STATES, Citadel Press, 1951. Reprinted by permission.

high degree of satisfaction. We expect great things from men who have made such a noble stand against the designs of their *fellow-men* to enslave them. We cannot but wish and hope Sir, that you will have the same grand object, we mean civil and religious liberty, in view in our next session. The divine spirit of *freedom*, seems to fire every humane breast on this continent, except such as are bribed to assist in executing the execrable plan.

We are very sensible that it would be highly detrimental to our present masters, if we were allowed to demand all that of *right* belongs to us for past services; this we disclaim. Even the *Spaniards*, who have not those sublime ideas of freedom that English men have, are conscious that they have no right to all the services of their fellow-men, we mean the *Africans*, whom they have purchased with their money; therefore they allow them one day in a week to work for themselves, to enable them to earn money to purchase the residue of their time, which they have a right to demand in such portions as they are able to pay for (a due appraizement of their services being first made, which always stands at the purchase money). We do not pretend to dictate to you Sir, or to the Honorable Assembly, of which you are a member. We acknowledge our obligations to you for what you have already done, but as the people of this province seem to be actuated by the principles of equity and justice, we cannot but expect your house will again take our deplorable case into serious consideration, and give us that ample relief from, *as men*, we have a natural right to.

But since the wise and righteous governor of the universe, has permitted our fellow men to make us slaves, we bow in submission to him, and determine to behave in such a manner as that we may have reason to expect the divine approbation of, and assistance in, our peaceable and lawful attempts to gain our freedom.

We are willing to submit to such regulations and laws, as may be made relative to us, until we leave the province, which we determine to do as soon as we can, from our joynt labours procure money to transport ourselves to some part of the Coast of *Africa*, where we propose a settlement. We are very desirous that you should have instructions relative to us, from your town, therefore we pray you to communicate this letter to them, and ask this favor for us.

In behalf of our fellow slaves in this province, and by order of their Committee.
Peter Bestes, Sambo Freeman, Felix Holbrook, Chester Joie.

For the Representative of the town of Thompson.

Declaration and Resolves of the First Continental Congress

In September 1774, delegates representing all the colonies except Georgia met in Philadelphia. They formed the First Continental Congress and published a declaration asking England for a repeal of some acts of Parliament passed since 1763. Part of this document is reprinted below.

Whereas, Since the close of the last war, the British Parliament, claiming a power of right to bind the people of America by statute in all cases whatsoever, hath in some acts expressly imposed taxes on them, and in others, under various pretenses, but in fact for the purpose of raising a revenue, hath imposed rates and duties payable in these colonies, established a board of commissioners with unconstitutional powers, and extended the jurisdiction of courts of admiralty not only for collecting the said duties, but for the trial of causes merely arising within the body of a county.

And whereas, In consequence of other statutes, judges who before held only estates at will in their offices have been made dependent on the Crown alone for their salaries; and standing armies kept in times of peace. And it has lately been resolved in Parliament that by force of a statute made in the thirty-fifth year of the reign of King Henry the Eighth, colonists may be transported to England and tried there upon accusations for treasons and misprisions, or concealments of treasons committed in the colonies; and by a late statute, such trials have been directed in cases therein mentioned.

And whereas, In the last session of Parliament, three statutes were made . . . . All which statutes are impolitic, unjust, and cruel, as well as unconstitutional, and most dangerous and destructive of American rights.

And whereas, Assemblies have been frequently dissolved, contrary to the rights of the people, when they attempted to deliberate on grievances; and their dutiful, humble, loyal, and reasonable petitions to the Crown for redress have been repeatedly treated with contempt by His Majesty's ministers of state:

The good people of the several colonies of New Hampshire, Massachusetts Bay, Rhode Island and Providence Plantations, Connecticut, New York, New Jersey, Pennsylvania, Newcastle, Kent and Sussex on Delaware, Maryland, Virginia, North Carolina, and South Carolina, justly alarmed at these arbitrary proceedings of Parliament and administration, have severally elected, constituted, and appointed deputies to meet and sit in general congress, in the city of Philadelphia, in order to obtain such establishment as that their religion, laws, and liberties may not be subverted:

Whereupon the deputies so appointed being now assembled, in a full and free representation of these colonies, taking into their most serious consideration the best means of attaining the ends aforesaid, do in the first place, as Englishmen their ancestors in like cases have usually done, for asserting and vindicating their rights and liberties, declare,

That the inhabitants of the English colonies in North America, by the immutable laws of nature, the principles of the English constitution, and the several charters or compacts, have the following rights:

Resolved, ...

1. That they are entitled to life, liberty, and property, and they have never ceded to any sovereign power whatever a right to dispose of either without their consent.

2. That our ancestors, who first settled these colonies, were, at the time of their emigration from the mother country, entitled to all the rights, liberties, and immunities of free and natural-born subjects within the realm of England.

3. That by such emigration they by no means forfeited, surrendered, or lost any of those rights, but that they were, and their descendants now are, entitled to the exercise and enjoyment of all such of them as their local and other circumstances enable them to exercise and enjoy.

4. That the foundation of English liberty, and of all free government, is a right in the people to participate in their legislative council: and as the English colonists are not represented, and from their local and other circumstances, cannot properly be represented in the British Parliament, they are entitled to a free and exclusive power of legislation in their several provincial legislatures, where their right of representation can alone be preserved, in all cases of taxation and internal polity, subject only to the negative of their sovereign, in such manner as has been heretofore used and accustomed. But, from the necessity of the case, and a regard to the mutual interest of both countries, we cheerfully consent to the operation of such acts of the British Parliament as are bona fide restrained to the regulation of our external commerce, for the purpose of securing the commercial advantages of the whole empire to the mother country, and the commercial benefits of its respective members, excluding every idea of taxation, internal or external, for raising a revenue on the subjects in America without their consent.

5. That the respective colonies are entitled to the common law of England, and more especially to the

great and inestimable privilege of being tried by their peers of the vicinage, according to the course of that law.

6. That they are entitled to the benefit of such of the English statutes as existed at the time of their colonization; and which they have, by experience, respectively found to be applicable to their several local and other circumstances.

7. That these, His Majesty's colonies, are likewise entitled to all the immunities and privileges granted and confirmed to them by royal charters, or secured by their several codes of provincial laws.

8. That they have a right peaceably to assemble, consider of their grievances, and petition the King; and that all prosecutions, prohibitory proclamations, and commitments for the same, are illegal.

9. That the keeping a standing army in these colonies, in times of peace, without the consent of the legislature of that colony in which such army is kept, is against law.

10. It is indispensably necessary to good government, and rendered essential by the English constitution, that the constituent branches of the legislature be independent of each other; that, therefore, the exercise of legislative power in several colonies, by a council appointed during pleasure, by the Crown, is unconstitutional, dangerous, and destructive to the freedom of American legislation.

All and each of which the aforesaid deputies, in behalf of themselves, and their constituents, do claim, demand, and insist on, as their indubitable rights and liberties; which cannot be legally taken from them, altered or abridged by any power whatever, without their own consent, by their representatives in their several provincial legislatures.

In the course of our inquiry, we find many infringements and violations of the foregoing rights, which, from an ardent desire that harmony and mutual intercourse of affection and interest may be restored, we pass over for the present, and proceed to state such acts and measures as have been adopted since the last war, which demonstrate a system formed to enslave America.

Resolved, That the following acts of Parliament are infringements and violations of the rights of the colonists; and that the repeal of them is essentially necessary, in order to restore harmony between Great Britain and the American colonies, viz.:

The several Acts ... which impose duties for the purpose of raising a revenue in America, extend the powers of the admiralty courts beyond their ancient limits, deprive the American subject of trial by jury, authorize the judges' certificate to indemnify the prosecutor from damages that he might otherwise be liable to, requiring oppressive security from a claimant of ships and goods seized before he shall be allowed to defend his property; and are subversive of American rights.

Also the 12 Geo. III, ch. 24, entitled "An act for the better securing His Majesty's dockyards, magazines, ships, ammunition, and stores," which declares a new offense in America, and deprives the American subject of a constitutional trial by a jury of the vicinage, by authorizing the trial of any person charged with the committing any offense described in the said act, out of the realm, to be indicted and tried for the same in any shire or county within the realm.

Also the three acts passed in the last session of Parliament, for stopping the port and blocking up the harbor of Boston, for altering the charter and government of the Massachusetts Bay, and that which is entitled "An Act for the better administration of Justice," etc.

Also the act passed the same session for establishing the Roman Catholic religion in the province of Quebec, abolishing the equitable system of English laws, and erecting a tyranny there, to the great danger, from so great a dissimilarity of religion, law, and government, of the neighboring British colonies, by the assistance of whose blood and treasure the said country was conquered from France.

Also the act passed the same session for the better providing suitable quarters for officers and soldiers in His Majesty's service in North America.

Also, that the keeping a standing army in several of these colonies, in time of peace, without the consent of the legislature of that colony in which the army is kept, is against law.

To these grievous acts and measures Americans cannot submit; but in hopes that their fellow-subjects in Great Britain will, on a revision of them restore us to that state in which both countries found happiness and prosperity, we have for the present only resolved to pursue the following peaceable measures: (1) To enter into a nonimportation, nonconsumption, and nonexportation agreement or association. (2) To prepare an address to the people of Great Britain, and a memorial to the inhabitants of British America, and (3) To prepare a loyal address to His Majesty, agreeable to resolutions already entered into.

A Call for Independence

Thomas Paine is considered to be one of the great revolutionists of the late eighteenth century. He emigrated to America from England in 1774 and began writing a series of articles, the most popular of which was entitled *Common Sense* (1776). With a great deal of enthusiasm and simple logic which all the people could understand, Paine promoted a powerful argument supporting American independence.*

... Leaving the moral part to private reflection, I shall chiefly confine my farther remarks to the following heads:

First, That it is the interest of America to be seperated from Britain.

Secondly, Which is the easiest and most practicable plan, reconciliation or independance? with some occasional remarks.

In support of the first, I could, if I judged it proper, produce the opinion of some of the ablest and most experienced men on this continent; and whose sentiments, on that head, are not yet publicly known. It is in reality a self-evident position: For no nation, in a state of foreign dependance, limited in its commerce, and cramped and fettered in its legislative powers, can ever arrive at any material eminence. America doth not yet know what opulence is; and although the progress which she hath made, stands unparalleled in the history of other nations, it is but childhood, compared with what she would be capable of arriving at, had she, as she ought to have, the legislative powers in her own hands. England is, at this time, proudly coveting what would do her no good, were she to accomplish it; and the continent hesitating on a matter, which will be her final ruin if neglected. It is the commerce, and not the conquest of America, by which England is to be benefited, and that would in a great measure continue, were the countries as independant of each other as France and Spain; because in many articles, neither can go to a better market. But it is the independance of this country on Britain or any other, which is now the main and only object worthy of contention, and which, like all other truths discovered by necessity, will appear clearer and stronger every day.

First. Because it will come to that one time or other.

Secondly. Because the longer it is delayed, the harder it will be to accomplish.

I have frequently amused myself both in public and private companies, with silently remarking the specious errors of those who speak without reflecting. And among the many which I have heard, the following seems the most general, viz. that had this rupture happened forty or fifty years hence, instead of *now*, the Continent would have been more able to have

shaken off the dependance. To which I reply, that our military ability *at this time*, arises from the experience gained in the late war, and which in forty or fifty years time, would have been totally extinct. ...

Should affairs be patched up with Britain, and she to remain the governing and sovereign power of America, (which as matters are now circumstanced, is giving up the point entirely) we shall deprive ourselves of the very means of sinking the debt we have, or may contract. The value of the back lands, which some of the provinces are clandestinely deprived of, by the unjust extension of the limits of Canada, valued only at five pounds sterling per hundred acres, amount to upwards of twenty five millions, Pennsylvania currency; and the quit-rents at one penny sterling per acre, to two millions yearly. ...

I proceed now to the second head, viz. Which is the easiest and most practicable plan, *Reconciliation or Independence;* with some occasional remarks.

He who takes nature for his guide, is not easily beaten out of his argument, and on that ground I answer *generally, That* Independance *being a* single simple line, *contained within ourselves; and reconciliation, a matter exceedingly perplexed and complicated, and in which, a treacherous capricious court is to interfere, gives the answer without a doubt.*

The present state of America is truly alarming to every man who is capable of reflection. Without law, without government, without any other mode of power than what is founded on, and granted by courtesy. Held together by an unexampled concurrence of sentiment, which, is nevertheless subject to change, and which, every secret enemy is endeavouring to dissolve. Our present condition, is, Legislation without law; wisdom without a plan; a constitution without a name; and, what is strangely astonishing, perfect Independance, contending for dependance. The instance is without a precedent; the case never existed before; and who can tell what may be the event? The property of no man is secure in the present unbraced system of things. The mind of the multitude is left at random, and seeing no fixed object before them, they pursue such as fancy or opinion starts. Nothing is criminal; there is no such thing as treason; wherefore, every one thinks himself at liberty to act as he pleases. The Tories would not have dared to assemble offensively, had they known that their lives, by that act, were forfeited to the laws of the state. A line of distinction should be drawn, between English soldiers taken in battle, and inhabitants of America taken in arms. The first are prisoners, but the latter traitors. The one forfeits his liberty, the other his head. ...

Put us, say some, upon the footing we were on in sixty-three. ... To be on the footing of sixty-three, it

---

*Appendix to *Common Sense* by Thomas Paine.

is not sufficient, that the laws only be put on the same state, but that our circumstances, likewise be put on the same state; our burnt and destroyed towns repaired or built up, our private losses made good, our public debts (contracted for defence) discharged; otherwise we shall be millions worse than we were at that enviable period. Such a request, had it been complied with a year ago, would have won the heart and soul of the Continent, but now it is too late. "The Rubicon is passed."

Besides, the taking up arms, merely to enforce the repeal of a pecuniary law, seems as unwarrantable by the divine law, and as repugnant to human feelings, as the taking up arms to enforce the obedience thereto. The object, on either side, doth not justify the means; for the lives of men are too valuable, to be cast away on such trifles. It is the violence which is done and threatened to our persons; the destruction of our property by an armed force; the invasion of our country by fire and sword, which conscientiously qualifies the use of arms: And the instant, in which such a mode of defence became necessary, all subjection to Britain ought to have ceased; and the independancy of America, should have been considered, as dating its æra from, and published by, *the first musket that was fired against her.* This line is a line of consistency; neither drawn by caprice, nor extended by ambition; but produced by a chain of events, of which the colonies were not the authors.

I shall conclude these remarks, with the following timely and well intended hint. We ought to reflect, that there are three different ways, by which an independancy may hereafter be effected; and that *one* of those *three*, will one day or other, be the fate of America, viz. By the legal voice of the people in Congress; by a military power; or by a mob: It may not always happen that our soldiers are citizens, and the multitude a body of reasonable men; vertue, as I have already remarked, is not hereditary, neither is it perpetual. Should an independancy be brought about by the first of those means, we have every opportunity and every encouragement before us, to form the noblest purest constitution on the face of the earth. We have it in our power to begin the world over again. A situation, similar to the present, hath not happened since the days of Noah until now. The birth day of a new world is at hand, and a race of men, perhaps as numerous as all Europe contains, are to receive their portion of freedom from the event of a few months. The reflection is awful and in this point of view, how trifling, how ridiculous, do the little paltry cavillings, of a few weak or interested men appear, when weighed against the business of a world. . . .

In short, Independance is the only BOND that can tye and keep us together. We shall then see our object, and our ears will be legally shut against the schemes of an intriguing, as well as a cruel enemy. We shall then too be on a proper footing to treat with Britain; for there is reason to conclude, that the pride of that court will be less hurt by treating with the American states for terms of peace, than with those she denominates "rebellious subjects," for terms of accommodation. It is our delaying it that encourages her to hope for conquest, and our backwardness tends only to prolong the war. As we have, without any good effect therefrom, withheld our trade to obtain a redress of our grievances, let us now try the alternative, by *independantly* redressing them ourselves, and then offering to open the trade. The mercantile and reasonable part in England will be still with us; because, peace with trade, is preferable to war without it. And if this offer is not accepted, other courts may be applied to. On these grounds I rest the matter. And as no offer hath yet been made to refute the doctrine contained in the former editions of this pamphlet, it is a negative proof, that either the doctrine cannot be refuted, or, that the party in favour of it are too numerous to be opposed. *Wherefore,* instead of gazing at each other with suspicious or doubtful curiosity, let each of us hold out to his neighbour the hearty hand of friendship, and unite in drawing a line, which, like an act of oblivion, shall bury in forgetfulness every former dissention. Let the names of Whig and Tory be extinct; and let none other be heard among us, than those of *a good citizen, an open and resolute friend, and a virtuous supporter of the rights of mankind and of the free and independant states of America.*

Mercantilism

Adam Smith (1723-1790) was a professor and apostle of liberalism in economics. His major work, *An Inquiry into the Nature and Causes of the Wealth of Nations,* was written in 1776 and became the major treatise on free enterprise and the competitive system. In this work, Smith defined mercantilism as the policy which kept the trade and wealth of a country's colonies in its own hands. Dissatisfaction with English mercantilism became an important reason for the American colonists' fight for independence from their mother country.*

---

*Adam Smith, AN INQUIRY INTO THE NATURE AND CAUSES OF THE WEALTH OF NATIONS, G. P. Putnam Sons, 1904.

OF THE PRINCIPLE OF THE COMMERCIAL OR MERCANTILE SYSTEM

That wealth consists in money, or in gold and silver, is a popular notion which naturally arises from the double function of money, as the instrument of commerce, and as the measure of value. In consequence of its being the instrument of commerce, when we have money we can more readily obtain whatever else we have occasion for, than by means of any other commodity. The great affair, we always find, is to get money. When that is obtained, there is no difficulty in making any subsequent purchase. In consequence of its being the measure of value, we estimate that of all other commodities by the quantity of money which they will exchange for. We say of a rich man that he is worth a great deal, and of a poor man that he is worth very little money. A frugal man, or a man eager to be rich, is said to love money; and a careless, a generous, or a profuse man is said to be indifferent about it. To grow rich is to get money; and wealth and money, in short, are, in common language, considered as in every respect synonymous.

A rich country, in the same manner as a rich man, is supposed to be a country abounding in money; and to heap up gold and silver in any country is supposed to be the readiest way to enrich it. For some time after the discovery of America, the first enquiry of the Spaniards, when they arrived upon any unknown coast, used to be, if there was any gold or silver to be found in the neighbourhood? By the information which they received, they judged whether it was worth while to make a settlement there, or if the country was worth the conquering. Plano Carpino, a monk sent ambassador from the king of France to one of the sons of the famous Gengis Khan, says that the Tartars used frequently to ask him, if there was plenty of sheep and oxen in the kingdom of France? Their enquiry had the same object with that of the Spaniards. They wanted to know if the country was rich enough to be worth the conquering. Among the Tartars, as among all other nations of shepherds, who are generally ignorant of the use of money, cattle are the instruments of commerce and the measures of value. Wealth, therefore, according to them, consisted in cattle, as according to the Spaniards it consisted in gold and silver....

Others admit that if a nation could be separated from all the world, it would be of no consequence how much, or how little money circulated in it. The consumable goods which were circulated by means of this money, would only be exchanged for a greater or a smaller number of pieces; but the real wealth or poverty of the country, they allow, would depend altogether upon the abundance or scarcity of these consumable goods. But it is otherwise, they think, with countries which have connections with foreign nations, and which are obliged to carry on foreign wars, and to maintain fleets and armies in distant countries. This, they say, cannot be done, but by sending abroad, money to pay them with; and a nation cannot send much money abroad, unless it has a good deal at home. Every such nation, therefore, must endeavour in time of peace to accumulate gold and silver, that, when occasion requires, it may have wherewithal to carry on foreign wars.

In consequence of these popular notions, all the different nations of Europe have studied, though to little purpose, every possible means of accumulating gold and silver in their respective countries. Spain and Portugal, the proprietors of the principal mines which supply Europe with those metals, have either prohibited their exportation under the severest penalties, or subjected it to a considerable duty....

When those countries became commercial, the merchants found this prohibition, upon many occasions, extremely inconvenient. They could frequently buy more advantageously with gold and silver than with any other commodity, the foreign goods which they wanted, either to import into their own, or to carry to some other foreign country....

They represented, secondly, that this prohibition could not hinder the exportation of gold and silver, which, on account of the smallness of their bulk in proportion to their value, could easily be smuggled abroad. That this exportation could only be prevented by a proper attention to, what they called the balance of trade. That when the country exported to a greater value than it imported, a balance became due to it from foreign nations, which was necessarily paid to it in gold and silver, and thereby increased the quantity of those metals in the kingdom....

The two principles being established, however, that wealth consisted in gold and silver, and that those metals could be brought into a country which had no mines only by the balance of trade, or by exporting to a greater value than it imported; it necessarily became the great object of political economy to diminish as much as possible the importation of foreign goods for home consumption, and to increase as much as possible the exportation of the produce of domestic industry. Its two great engines for enriching the country, therefore, were restraints upon importation, and encouragements to exportation.

The restraints upon importation were of two kinds.

First, Restraints upon the importation of such foreign goods for home consumption as could be produced at home, from whatever country they were imported.

Secondly, Restraints upon the importation of goods of almost all kinds from those particular countries with which the balance of trade was supposed to be disadvantageous.

Those different restraints consisted sometimes in high duties, and sometimes in absolute prohibitions.

Exportation was encouraged sometimes by drawbacks, sometimes by bounties, sometimes by advantageous treaties of commerce with foreign states, and sometimes by the establishment of colonies in distant countries.

Drawbacks were given upon two different occasions. When the home-manufactures were subject to any duty or excise, either the whole or a part of it was frequently drawn back upon their exportation; and when foreign goods liable to a duty were imported in order to be exported again, either the whole or a part of this duty was sometimes given back upon such exportation.

Bounties were given for the encouragement either of some beginning manufactures, or of such sorts of industry of other kinds as were supposed to deserve particular favour.

By advantageous treaties of commerce, particular privileges were procured in some foreign state for the goods and merchants of the country, beyond what were granted to those of other countries.

By the establishment of colonies in distant countries, not only particular privileges, but a monopoly was frequently procured for the goods and merchants of the country which established them.

* * *

The Articles of Confederation

The problem of organizing a central government became the work of the delegates to the Second Continental Congress. They approved and adopted the Articles of Confederation in 1777 which loosely unified the colonies under one central government for the first time. However, the Articles contained many weaknesses and after America won its independence from Great Britain, the colonial leaders began to consider the creation of a stronger federal government.

Whereas the Delegates of the United States of America in Congress assembled did on the fifteenth day of November in the year of our Lord One Thousand Seven Hundred and Seventy-seven, and in the Second Year of the Independence of America agree

to certain articles of Confederation and perpetual Union between the States of Newhampshire, Massachusetts-bay, Rhodeisland and Providence Plantations, Connecticut, New York, New Jersey, Pennsylvania, Delaware, Maryland, Virginia, North-Carolina, South-Carolina and Georgia in the Words following, viz.

Article I. The style of this confederacy shall be "The United States of America."

Article II. Each State retains its sovereignty, freedom and independence, and every power, jurisdiction and right, which is not by this confederation expressly delegated to the United States, in Congress assembled.

Article III. The said States hereby severally enter into a firm league of friendship with each other, for their common defense, the security of their liberties, and their mutual and general welfare, binding themselves to assist each other, against all force offered to, or attacks made upon them, or any of them, on account of religion, sovereignty, trade, or any other pretense whatever.

Article IV. The better to secure and perpetuate mutual friendship and intercourse among the people of the different States in this Union, the free inhabitants of each of these States, paupers, vagabonds and fugitives from justice excepted, shall be entitled to all privileges and immunities of free citizens in the several States; and the people of each State shall have free ingress and regress to and from any other State, and shall enjoy therein all the privileges of trade and commerce, subject to the same duties, impositions and restrictions as the inhabitants thereof respectively, provided that such restrictions shall not extend so far as to prevent the removal of property imported into any State, to any other state of which the owner is an inhabitant; provided also that no imposition, duties or restriction shall be laid by any State, on the property of the United States, or either of them.

If any Person guilty of, or charged with treason, felony, or other high misdemeanor in any State, shall flee from justice, and be found in any of the United States, he shall upon demand of the Governor or Executive power, of the State from which he fled, be delivered up and removed to the State having jurisdiction of his offense.

Full faith and credit shall be given in each of these States to the records, acts and judicial proceedings of the courts and magistrates of every other State.

Article V. . . . No State shall be represented in Congress by less than two, nor by more than seven members; and no person shall be capable of being a delegate for more than three years in any term of six years; nor shall any person, being a delegate, be capable of holding any office under the United States, for which he, or another for his benefit receives any salary, fees or emolument of any kind. . . .

* * *

In determining questions in the United States, in Congress assembled, each State shall have one vote.

Freedom of speech and debate in Congress shall not be impeached or questioned in any court, or place out of Congress, and the members of Congress shall be protected in their persons from arrests and imprisonments, during the time of their going to and from, and attendance on Congress, except for treason, felony, or breach of the peace.

Article VI. No State without the consent of the United States in Congress assembled, shall send any embassy to, or receive any embassy from, or enter into any conference, agreement, alliance or treaty with any king, prince or state; nor shall any person holding any office of profit or trust under the United States, or any of them, accept of any present, emolument, office or title of any kind whatever from any king, prince or foreign state; nor shall the United States in Congress assembled, or any of them, grant any title of nobility.

No two or more States shall enter into any treaty, confederation or alliance whatever between them, without the consent of the United States in Congress assembled, specifying accurately the purposes for which the same is to be entered into, and how long it shall continue.

No State shall lay any imposts or duties, which may interfere with any stipulations in treaties, entered into by the United States in Congress assembled, with any king, prince or state, in pursuance of any treaties already proposed by Congress, to the courts of France and Spain.

* * *

Article VIII. All charges of war, and all other expenses that shall be incurred for the common defense or general welfare, and allowed by the United States in Congress assembled, shall be defrayed out of a common treasury, which shall be supplied by the several States, in proportion to the value of all land within each State, granted to or surveyed for any person, as such land and the buildings and improvements thereon shall be estimated according to such mode as the United States in Congress assembled, shall from time to time direct and appoint.

The taxes for paying that proportion shall be laid and levied by the authority and direction of the Legislatures of the several States within the time agreed upon by the United States in Congress assembled.

Article IX. The United States in Congress assembled, shall have the sole and exclusive right and power of determining on peace and war, except in the cases mentioned in the sixth article; of sending and receiving ambassadors; entering into treaties and alliances, provided that no treaty of commerce shall be made whereby the legislative power of the respective States shall be restrained from imposing such imposts and duties on foreigners, as their own people are subjected to, or from prohibiting the exportation or importation of any species of goods or commodities whatsoever; of establishing rules for deciding in all cases, what captures on land or water shall be legal, and in what manner prizes taken by land or naval forces in the service of the United States shall be divided or appropriated; of granting letters of marque and reprisal in times of peace; appointing courts for the trial of piracies and felonies committed on the high seas and establishing courts for receiving and determining finally appeals in all cases of captures, provided that no member of Congress shall be appointed a judge of any of the said courts.

* * *

The United States in Congress assembled shall also have the sole and exclusive right and power of regulating the alloy and value of coin struck by their own authority, or by that of the respective States; fixing the standard of weights and measures throughout the United States; regulating the trade and managing all affairs with the Indians, not members of any of the States, provided that the legislative right of any State within its own limits be not infringed or violated; establishing and regulating post-offices from one State to another, throughout all the United States, and exacting such postage on the papers passing thro' the same as may be requisite to defray the expenses of the said office; appointing all officers of the land forces, in the service of the United States, excepting regimental officers; appointing all the officers of the naval forces, and commissioning all officers whatever in the service of the United States; making rules for the government and regulation of the said land and naval forces, and directing their operations.

* * *

The United States in Congress assembled shall never engage in a war, nor grant letters of marque and reprisal in time of peace, nor enter into any treaties or alliances, nor coin money, nor regulate the value thereof, nor ascertain the sums and expenses necessary for the defense and welfare of the United States, or any of them, nor emit bills, nor borrow money on the credit of the United States, nor appropriate money, nor agree upon the number of vessels of war, to be built or purchased, or the number of land or sea forces to be raised, nor appoint a commander in chief of the army or navy, unless nine States assent to the same; nor shall a question on any other point, except for adjourning from day to day be determined, unless by the votes of a majority of the United States in Congress assembled.

* * *

Article XI. Canada acceding to this confederation, and joining in the measures of the United States, shall be admitted into, and entitled to all the advantages of this Union; but no other colony shall be admitted into the same, unless such admission be agreed to by nine States.

Article XII. All bills of credit emitted, monies borrowed and debts contracted by, or under the authority of Congress, before the assembling of the United States, in pursuance of the present confederation, shall be deemed and considered as a charge against the United States, for payment and satisfaction whereof the said United States, and the public faith are hereby solemnly pledged.

Article XIII. Every State shall abide by the determinations of the United States in Congress assembled, on all questions which by this confederation are submitted to them. And the articles of this confederation shall be inviolably observed by every State, and the Union shall be perpetual; nor shall any alteration at any time hereafter be made in any of them; unless such alteration be agreed to in a Congress of the United States, and be afterwards confirmed by the Legislatures of every State.

And whereas it hath pleased the Great Governor of the World to incline the hearts of the Legislatures we respectively represent in Congress, to approve of, and to authorize us to ratify the said articles of confederation and perpetual union. Know ye that we the undersigned delegates, by virtue of the power and authority to us given for that purpose, do by these presents, in the name and in behalf of our respective constituents, fully and entirely ratify and confirm each and every of the said articles of confederation and perpetual union, and all and singular the matters and things therein contained: and we do further solemnly plight and engage the faith of our respective constituents, that they shall abide by the determinations of the United States in Congress assembled, on all questions, which by the said confederation are submitted to them. And that the articles thereof shall be inviolably observed by the States we respectively represent, and that the Union shall be perpetual.

In witness whereof we have hereunto set our hands in Congress. Done at Philadelphia in the State of Pennsylvania the ninth day of July in the year of our Lord one thousand seven hundred and seventy-eight, and in the third year of the independence of America.

The *Serapis* vs. the *Bon Homme Richard*—A Sea Fight

John Paul Jones was the naval hero of the American Revolution. Born in Scotland, he is best known for his famous words directed at Captain Pearson of the British ship *Serapis*: "I have not yet begun to fight."

After a three-hour period of combat and against great odds, John Paul Jones defeated the British man-of-war *Serapis* in 1779 only to have his own ship, the *Bon Homme Richard* sunk two days later.*

On the morning of that day, the 23d [September, 1779], the brig from Holland not being in sight, we chased a brigantine that appeared laying to, to windward. About noon, we saw and chased a large ship that appeared coming round Flamborough Head, from the northward, and at the same time I manned and armed one of the pilot boats to send in pursuit of the brigantine, which now appeared to be the vessel that I had forced ashore. Soon after this, a fleet of forty-one sail appeared off Flamborough Head, bearing N.N.E. This induced me to abandon the single ship which had then anchored in Burlington Bay; I also called back the pilot boat, and hoisted a signal for a general chase. When the fleet discovered us bearing down, all the merchant ships crowded sail towards the shore. The two ships of war that protected the fleet at the same time steered from the land, and made the disposition for battle. In approaching the enemy, I crowded every possible sail, and made the signal for the line of battle, to which the Alliance showed no attention. Earnest as I was for the action, I could not reach the commodore's ship until seven in the evening, being then within pistol shot, when he hailed the Bon Homme Richard. We answered him by firing a whole broadside.

The battle being thus begun, was continued with unremitting fury. Every method was practised on both sides to gain an advantage, and rake each other; and I must confess that the enemy's ship, being much more manageable than the Bon Homme Richard, gained thereby several times an advantageous situation, in spite of my best endeavours to prevent it. As

___

*The Serapis *vs. the* Bon Homme Richard, *A Sea Fight* by John Paul Jones.

I had to deal with an enemy of greatly superior force, I was under the necessity of closing with him, to prevent the advantage which he had over me in point of manœuvre. It was my intention to lay the Bon Homme Richard athwart the enemy's bow; but as that operation required great dexterity in the management of both sails and helm, and some of our braces being shot away, it did not exactly succeed to my wish. The enemy's bowsprit, however, came over the Bon Homme Richard's poop by the mizen-mast, and I made both ships fast together in that situation, which, by the action of the wind on the enemy's sails, forced her stern close to the Bon Homme Richard's bow, so that the ships lay square alongside of each other, the yards being all entangled, and the cannon of each ship touching the opponent's. When this position took place, it was eight o'clock, previous to which the Bon Homme Richard had received sundry eighteen-pound shots below the water, and leaked very much. My battery of twelve-pounders, on which I had placed my chief dependence, being commanded by Lieutenant Dale and Colonel Weibert, and manned principally with American seamen and French volunteers, was entirely silenced and abandoned. As to the six old eighteen-pounders that formed the battery of the lower gun-deck, they did no service whatever, except firing eight shot in all. Two out of three of them burst at the first fire, and killed almost all the men who were stationed to manage them. Before this time, too, Colonel de Chamillard, who commanded a party of twenty soldiers on the poop, had abandoned that station after having lost some of his men. I had now only two pieces of cannon, (nine-pounders,) on the quarter-deck, that were not silenced, and not one of the heavier cannon was fired during the rest of the action. The purser, M. Mease, who commanded the guns on the quarter-deck, being dangerously wounded in the head, I was obliged to fill his place, and with great difficulty rallied a few men, and shifted over one of the lee quarter-deck guns, so that we afterwards played three pieces of nine-pounders upon the enemy. The tops alone seconded the fire of this little battery, and held out bravely during the whole of the action, especially the main-top, where Lieutenant Stack commanded. I directed the fire of one of the three cannon against the main-mast, with double-headed shot, while the other two were exceedingly well served with grape and canister shot, to silence the enemy's musketry and clear her decks, which was at last effected. The enemy were, as I have since understood, on the instant of calling for quarter, when the cowardice or treachery of three of my under-officers induced them to call to the enemy. The English commodore asked me if I demanded

quarter, and I having answered him in the most determined negative, they renewed the battle with double fury. They were unable to stand the deck; but the fire of their cannon, especially the lower battery, which was entirely formed of ten-pounders, was incessant; both ships were set on fire in various places, and the scene was dreadful beyond the reach of language. To account for the timidity of my three under-officers, I mean, the gunner, the carpenter, and the master-at-arms, I must observe, that the two first were slightly wounded, and, as the ship had received various shot under water, and one of the pumps being shot away, the carpenter expressed his fears that she would sink, and the other two concluded that she was sinking, which occasioned the gunner to run aft on the poop, without my knowledge, to strike the colours. Fortunately for me, a cannon ball had done that before, by carrying away the ensign-staff; he was therefore reduced to the necessity of sinking, as he supposed, or of calling for quarter, and he preferred the latter.

All this time the Bon Homme Richard had sustained the action alone, and the enemy, though much superior in force, would have been very glad to have got clear, as appears by their own acknowledgments, and by their having let go an anchor the instant that I laid them on board, by which means they would have escaped, had I not made them well fast to the Bon Homme Richard. . . .

. . . My situation was really deplorable; the Bon Homme Richard received various shot under water from the Alliance; the leak gained on the pumps, and the fire increased much on board both ships. Some officers persuaded me to strike, of whose courage and good sense I entertain a high opinion. My treacherous master-at-arms let loose all my prisoners without my knowledge, and my prospects became gloomy indeed. I would not, however, give up the point. The enemy's main-mast began to shake, their firing decreased fast, ours rather increased, and the British colours were struck at half an hour past ten o'clock.

This prize proved to be the British ship of war the Serapis, a new ship of forty-four guns, built on the most approved construction, with two complete batteries, one of them of eighteen-pounders, and commanded by the brave Commodore Richard Pearson. I had yet two enemies to encounter, far more formidable than the Britons, I mean, fire and water. The Serapis was attacked only by the first, but the Bon Homme Richard was assailed by both; there was five feet water in the hold, and though it was moderate from the explosion of so much gunpowder, yet the three pumps that remained could with difficulty only keep the water from gaining. The fire broke out in various parts of the ship, in spite of all the water that could be thrown in to quench it, and at length broke out as low as the powder magazine, and within a few inches of the powder. In that dilemma, I took out the powder upon deck, ready to be thrown overboard at the last extremity, and it was ten o'clock the next day, the 24th, before the fire was entirely extinguished. With respect to the situation of the Bon Homme Richard, the rudder was cut entirely off, the stern frame and transoms were almost entirely cut away, and the timbers by the lower deck, especially from the main-mast towards the stern, being greatly decayed with age, were mangled beyond my power of description, and a person must have been an eye witness to form a just idea of the tremendous scene of carnage, wreck, and ruin, which every where appeared. Humanity cannot but recoil from the prospect of such finished horror, and lament that war should be capable of producing such fatal consequences. . . .

. . . The wind augmented in the night, and the next day, the 25th, so that it was impossible to prevent the good old ship from sinking. They did not abandon her till after nine o'clock; the water was then up to the lower deck, and a little after ten I saw, with inexpressible grief, the last glimpse of *the Bon Homme Richard.* No lives were lost with the ship, but it was impossible to save the stores of any sort whatever. I lost even the best part of my clothes, books, and papers; and several of my officers lost all their clothes and effects.

Alexander Hamilton Supports the Role of Negroes in the American Revolution

In a letter written in 1779, Alexander Hamilton displays a desire for more Negroes to fight in the Revolution. He points out that there are false prejudices and misconception of Negroes which must be overcome so that they can make a greater contribution to the common cause and in doing so, perhaps pave the way for their emancipation.

Head-quarters, March 14th, 1779.

DEAR SIR,

Colonel Laurens, who will have the honour of delivering you this letter, is on his way to South Carolina, on a project which I think, in the present situation of affairs there, is a very good one, and deserves every kind of support and encouragement.

This is to raise two, three, or four battalions of negroes, with the assistance of the government of that State, by contributions from the owners, in proportion to the number they possess. If you should think proper to enter upon the subject with him, he will give you a detail of his plan. He wishes to have it recommended by Congress to the State; and, as an inducement, that they would engage to take those battalions into continental pay.

It appears to me that an expedient of this kind, in the present state of southern affairs, is the most rational that can be adopted, and promises very important advantages. Indeed, I hardly see how a sufficient force can be collected in that quarter without it; and the enemy's operations there are growing infinitely serious and formidable. I have not the least doubt that the negroes will make very excellent soldiers with proper management; and I will venture to pronounce that they cannot be put into better hands than those of Mr. Laurens. He has all the zeal, intelligence, enterprise, and every other qualification necessary to succeed in such an undertaking. It is a maxim with some great military judges, that with sensible officers, soldiers can hardly be too stupid; and, on this principle, it is thought that the Russians would make the best troops in the world, if they were under other officers than their own. The King of Prussia is among the number who maintain this doctrine, and has a very emphatical saying on the occasion, which I do not exactly recollect. I mention this, because I hear it frequently objected to the scheme of imbodying negroes, that they are too stupid to make soldiers. This is so far from appearing to me a valid objection, that I think their want of cultivation (for their natural faculties are probably as good as ours), joined to that habit of subordination, which they acquire from a life of servitude, will make them sooner become soldiers than our white inhabitants. Let officers be men of sense and sentiment, and the nearer the soldiers approach to machines, perhaps the better.

I foresee that this project will have to combat much opposition from prejudice and self-interest. The contempt we have been taught to entertain for the blacks, makes us fancy many things that are founded neither in reason nor experience; and an unwillingness to part with property of so valuable a kind, will furnish a thousand arguments to show the impracticability, or pernicious tendency, of a scheme which requires such a sacrifice. But it should be considered, that if we do not make use of them in this way, the enemy probably will; and that the best way to counteract the temptations they will hold out, will be to offer them ourselves. An essential part of the plan is to give them their freedom with their muskets. This will secure their fidelity, animate their courage, and, I believe, will have a good influence upon those who remain, by opening a door to their emancipation. This circumstance, I confess, has no small weight in inducing me to wish the success of the project; for the dictates of humanity and true policy equally interest me in favour of this unfortunate class of men.

With the truest respect and esteem,

I am, sir your most obedient servant,

ALEX. HAMILTON.

The Land Ordinance of 1785

The Land Ordinance of 1785 provided a systematic solution for the development of the western territory. It provided that money from sale of public lands would go to the United States government. It eliminated boundary disputes between states. Under this ordinance, towns were laid out in townships and one section in each township was to be set aside for education.*

Be it ordained by the United States in congress assembled, That the territory ceded by individual states, to the United States, which has been purchased of the Indian inhabitants, shall be disposed of in the following manner:

* * *

The surveyors, as they are respectively qualified, shall proceed to divide the said territory into townships of six miles square. . . .

* * *

The plats of the townships, respectively, shall be marked, by subdivisions, into lots of one mile square, or 640 acres . . . and numbered from 1 to 36. . . .

* * *

The board of treasury shall . . . proceed to sell the townships or fractional parts of townships, at public vendue . . . provided, that none of the lands within the said territory be sold under the price of one dollar the acre, to be paid in specie or loan office certificates . . . to be paid at the time of sales, on failure of which payment the said lands shall again be offered for sale.

There shall be reserved for the United States out

---

*Land Ordinance of 1785 in LAWS OF THE UNITED STATES OF AMERICA, published by John Biorea and W. John Duane, Philadelphia and R.C. Weightman, Washington, D.C., 1815.

of every township, the four lots, being numbered 8, 11, 26, 29, and out of every fractional part of a township, so many lots of the same numbers as shall be found thereon, for future sale. There shall be reserved the lot No. 16, of every township, for the maintenance of public schools within the said township; also, one-third part of all gold, silver, lead, and copper, mines, to be sold, or otherwise disposed of, as congress shall hereafter direct.

* * *

And be it further ordained, That three townships adjacent to lake Erie be reserved, to be hereafter disposed of by congress, for the use of the officers, men, and others, refugees from Canada, and the refugees from Nova Scotia, who are or may be entitled to grants of land. . . .

And be it further ordained, That the towns of Gnadenhutten, Schoenbrun, and Salem, on the Muskingum, and so much of the lands adjoining to the said towns, with the buildings and improvements thereon, shall be reserved for the sole use of the christian Indians, who were formerly settled there, or the remains of that society, as may, in the judgment of the geographer, be sufficient for them to cultivate.

Saving and reserving always, to all officers and soldiers entitled to lands on the northwest side of the Ohio, by donation or bounty from the commonwealth of Virginia, and to all persons claiming under them, all rights to which they are so entitled . . . be it ordained, that no part of the land included between the rivers called Little Miami and Scioto, on the northwest side of the river Ohio, be sold . . . until there shall first have been laid off and appropriated for the said officers and soldiers, and persons claiming under them, the lands they are entitled to. . . .

Done by the United States in congress assembled, the twentieth day of May, in the year of our Lord one thousand seven hundred and eighty-five, and of our sovereignty and independence the ninth.

RICHARD H. LEE, *president.*

On the Superiority
of Agriculture to Commerce

Thomas Jefferson, first secretary of state in the Washington cabinet, described his feelings on the moral superiority of agriculture to commerce in a private letter to John Jay on August 23, 1785. Jefferson believed that there was something inherently good, perhaps even godly, about farming and farmers. He wanted America to be a land of farmers, as opposed to Hamilton who welcomed commerce, industry, and manufacturing.*

To John Jay

(PRIVATE)

PARIS, August 23, 1785.

The present is occasioned by the question proposed in yours of June the 14th: "Whether it would be useful to us, to carry all our own productions, or none?"

Were we perfectly free to decide this question, I should reason as follows: We have now lands enough to employ an infinite number of people in their cultivation. Cultivators of the earth are the most valuable citizens. They are the most vigorous, the most independent, the most virtuous, and they are tied to their country, and wedded to its liberty and interests, by the most lasting bonds. As long, therefore, as they can find employment in this line, I would not convert them into mariners, artisans, or anything else. But our citizens will find employment in this line, till their numbers, and of course their productions, become too great for the demand, both internal and foreign. This is not the case as yet, and probably will not be for a considerable time. As soon as it is, the surplus of hands must be turned to something else. I should then, perhaps, wish to turn them to the sea in preference to manufactures; because, comparing the characters of the two classes, I find the former the most valuable citizens. I consider the class of artificers as the panders of vice, and the instruments by which the liberties of a country are generally overturned. However, we are not free to decide this question on principles of theory only. Our people are decided in the opinion that it is necessary for us to take a share in the occupation of the ocean, and their established habits induce them to require that the sea be kept open to them, and that that line of policy be pursued, which will render the use of that element to them as great as possible. I think it a duty in those intrusted with the administration of their affairs, to conform themselves to the decided choice of their constituents; and that, therefore, we should, in every instance, preserve an equality of right to them in the transportation of commodities, in the right of fishing, and in the other uses of the sea.

But what will be the consequence? Frequent wars without a doubt. Their property will be violated on the sea, and in foreign ports, their persons will be insulted, imprisoned, etc., for pretended debts, contracts, crimes, contraband, etc., etc. These insults must be resented, even if we had no feelings, yet to prevent their eternal repetition; or, in other words, our commerce on the ocean and in other countries, must be paid for by frequent war. The justest dispositions possible in ourselves, will not secure us against it. It would be necessary that all other nations were just also. Justice indeed, on our part, will save us from those wars which would have been produced by a contrary disposition. But how can we prevent those produced by the wrongs of other nations? By putting ourselves in a condition to punish them. Weakness provokes insult and injury, while a condition to punish, often prevents them. This reasoning leads to the necessity of some naval force; that being the only weapon by which we can reach an enemy. I think it to our interest to punish the first insult, because an insult unpunished is the parent of many others. We are not, at this moment, in a condition to do it, but we should put ourselves into it, as soon as possible. If a war with England should take place, it seems to me that the first thing necessary would be a resolution to abandon the carrying trade, because we cannot protect it. Foreign nations must, in that case, be invited to bring us what we want, and to take our productions in their own bottoms. This alone could prevent the loss of those productions to us, and the acquisition of them to our enemy. Our seamen might be employed in depredations on their trade. But how dreadfully we shall suffer on our coasts, if we have no force on the water, former experience has taught us. Indeed, I look forward with horror to the very possible case of war with a European power, and think there is no protection against them, but from the possession of some force on the sea. Our vicinity to their West India possessions, and to the fisheries, is a bridle which a small naval force, on our part, would hold in the mouths of the most powerful of these countries. I hope our land office will rid us of our debts, and that our first attention then, will be, to the beginning, a naval force of some sort. This alone can countenance our people as carriers on the water, and I suppose them to be determined to continue such.

Report on Manufactures

Thomas Jefferson and Alexander Hamilton found themselves on opposing sides on many issues. One of these was the issue of agriculture vs. manufacturing. The next reading is an excerpt from Hamilton's report on manufactures in 1791 in which he advocated

*Private Letter to John Jay on Superiority of Agriculture to Commerce by Thomas Jefferson in William Parker and Jonas Viles (eds.), LETTERS AND ADDRESSES OF THOMAS JEFFERSON, The National Jefferson Society, 1903.

America's economic independence from Europe through a system of diversified manufacturing.*

To affirm that the labor of the manufacturer is unproductive, because he consumes as much of the produce of land as he adds value to the raw material which he manufactures, is not better founded than it would be to affirm that the labor of the farmer which furnishes materials to the manufacturer, is unproductive, because he consumes an equal value of manufactured articles. Each furnishes a certain portion of the produce of his labor to the other, and each destroys a corresponding portion of the produce of the labor of the other. In the meantime, the maintenance of two citizens, instead of one, is going on; the State has two members instead of one; and they, together, consume twice the value of what is produced from the land.

If, instead of a farmer and artificer, there were a farmer only, he would be under the necessity of devoting a part of his labor to the fabrication of clothing and other articles, which he would procure of the artificer, in the case of there being such a person; and of course he would be able to devote less labor to the cultivation of his farm, and would draw from it a proportionately less product. The whole quantity of production, in this state of things, in provisions, raw materials, and manufactures, would certainly not exceed in value the amount of what would be produced in provisions and raw materials only, if there were an artificer as well as a farmer.

Again, if there were both an artificer and a farmer, the latter would be left at liberty to pursue exclusively the cultivation of his farm. A greater quantity of provisions and raw materials would, of course, be produced, equal, at least, as has been already observed, to the whole amount of the provisions, raw materials, and manufactures, which would exist on a contrary supposition. The artificer, at the same time, would be going on in the production of manufactured commodities, to an amount sufficient, not only to repay the farmer, in those commodities, for the provisions and materials which were procured from him, but to furnish the artificer himself with a supply of similar commodities for his own use. Thus, then, there would be two quantities or values in existence, instead of one; and the revenue and consumption would be double, in one case, what it would be in the other. . . .

It is now proper to proceed a step further, and to enumerate the principal circumstances from which it

may be inferred that manufacturing establishments not only occasion a positive augmentation of the produce and revenue of the society, but that they contribute essentially to rendering them greater than they could possibly be without such establishments. . . .

1. As to the division of labor.

It has justly been observed, that there is scarcely any thing of greater moment in the economy of a nation than the proper division of labor. The separation of occupations causes each to be carried to a much greater perfection than it could possibly acquire if they were blended. . . .

2. As to an extension of the use of machinery, a point which, though partly anticipated, requires to be placed in one or two additional lights.

The employment of machinery forms an item of great importance in the general mass of national industry. It is an artificial force brought in aid of the natural force of man; and, to all the purposes of labor, is an increase of hands, an accession of strength, unencumbered too by the expense of maintaining the laborer. May it not, therefore, be fairly inferred, that those occupations which give greatest scope to the use of this auxiliary, contribute most to the general stock of industrious effort, and, in consequence, to the general product of industry?

3. As to the additional employment of classes of the community not originally engaged in the particular business.

This is not among the least valuable of the means by which manufacturing institutions contribute to augment the general stock of industry and production. In places where those institutions prevail, besides the persons regularly engaged in them, they afford occasional and extra employment to industrious individuals and families, who are willing to devote the leisure resulting from the intermissions of their ordinary pursuits to collateral labors, as a resource for multiplying their acquisitions or their enjoyments. The husbandman himself experiences a new source of profit and support from the increased industry of his wife and daughters, invited and stimulated by the demands of the neighboring manufactories.

Besides this advantage of occasional employment to classes having different occupations, there is another, of a nature allied to it, and of a similar tendency. This is the employment of persons who would otherwise be idle, and in many cases a burthen on the community, either from the bias of temper, habit, infirmity of body, or some other cause, indisposing or disqualifying them for the toils of the country. It is worthy of particular remark that, in general, women

*Report on Manufactures, Dec. 5, 1791. WORKS OF ALEXANDER HAMILTON, Vol. IV.

and children are rendered more useful, and the latter more early useful, by manufacturing establishments, than they would otherwise be. . . .

4. As to the promoting of emigration from foreign countries.

Men reluctantly quit one course of occupation and livelihood for another, unless invited to it by very apparent and proximate advantages. Many who would go from one country to another, if they had a prospect of continuing with more benefit the callings to which they have been educated, will often not be tempted to change their situation by the hope of doing better in some other way. . . .

5. As to the furnishing greater scope for the diversity of talents and dispositions, which discriminate men from each other.

This is a much more powerful means of augmenting the fund of national industry, than may at first sight appear. It is a just observation, that minds of the strongest and most active powers for their proper objects, fall below mediocrity, and labor without effect, if confined to uncongenial pursuits. And it is thence to be inferred, that the results of human exertion may be immensely increased by diversifying its objects. When all the different kinds of industry obtain in a community, each individual can find his proper element, and can call into activity the whole vigor of his nature. . . .

6. As to the affording a more ample and various field for enterprise.

This also is of greater consequence in the general scale of national exertion than might, perhaps, on a superficial view be supposed, and has effects not altogether dissimilar from those of the circumstance last noticed. To cherish and stimulate the activity of the human mind, by multiplying the objects of enterprise, is not among the least considerable of the expedients by which the wealth of a nation may be promoted. Even things in themselves not positively advantageous sometimes become so, by their tendency to provoke exertion. . . .

7. As to the creating, in some instances, a new, and securing, in all, a more certain and steady demand for the surplus produce of the soil.

This is among the most important of the circumstances which have been indicated. It is a principal means by which the establishment of manufactures contributes to an augmentation of the produce or revenue of a country, and has an immediate and direct relation to the prosperity of agriculture. . . .

Considering how fast and how much the progress of new settlements in the United States must increase the surplus produce of the soil, and weighing seriously the tendency of the system which prevails among most of the commercial nations of Europe, whatever dependence may be placed on the force of natural circumstances to counteract the effects of an artificial policy, there appear strong reasons to regard the foreign demand for that surplus as too uncertain a reliance, and to desire a substitute for it in an extensive domestic market.

To secure such a market there is no other expedient than to promote manufacturing establishments. Manufacturers, who constitute the most numerous class, after the cultivators of land, are for that reason the principal consumers of the surplus of their labor. . . .

. . . The importations of manufactured supplies seem invariably to drain the merely agricultural people of their wealth. Let the situation of the manufacturing countries of Europe be compared, in this particular, with that of countries which only cultivate, and the disparity will be striking. Other causes, it is true, help to account for this disparity between some of them; and among these causes, the relative state of agriculture; but between others of them, the most prominent circumstance of dissimilitude arises from the comparative state of manufactures. . . .

One more point of view only remains, in which to consider the expediency of encouraging manufactures in the United States.

It is not uncommon to meet with an opinion, that, though the promoting of manufactures may be the interest of a part of the Union, it is contrary to that of another part. The Northern and Southern regions are sometimes represented as having adverse interests in this respect. Those are called manufacturing, these agricultural States; and a species of opposition is imagined to subsist between manufacturing and agricultural interests.

This idea of an opposition between those two interests is the common error of the early periods of every country; but experience gradually dissipates it. Indeed, they are perceived so often to succor and befriend each other, that they come at length to be considered as one—a supposition which has been frequently abused, and is not universally true. Particular encouragements of particular manufactures may be of a nature to sacrifice the interests of landholders to those of manufacturers; but it is nevertheless a maxim, well established by experience, and generally acknowledged, where there has been sufficient experience, that the aggregate prosperity of manufactures and the aggregate prosperity of agriculture are intimately connected. In the course of the discussion which has had place, various weighty considerations have been adduced, operating in support of that maxim. Perhaps the superior steadiness of the demand of a domestic market, for the surplus produce of the soil, is, alone, a convincing argument of its truth.

* * *

In order to make a better judgment of the means proper to be resorted to by the United States, it will be of use to advert to those which have been employed with success in other countries. The principal of these are:

1. Protecting duties—or duties on those foreign articles which are the rivals of the domestic ones intended to be encouraged.

Duties of this nature evidently amount to a virtual bounty on the domestic fabrics; since, by enhancing the charges on foreign articles, they enable the national manufacturers to undersell all their foreign competitors. . . .

2. Prohibitions of rival articles, or duties equivalent to prohibitions.

This is another and an efficacious mean of encouraging national manufactures; but, in general, it is only fit to be employed when a manufacture has made such progress, and is in so many hands, as to insure a due competition, and an adequate supply on reasonable terms. Of duties equivalent to prohibitions, there are examples in the laws of the United States. . . .

3. Prohibitions of the exportation of the materials of manufactures.

The desire of securing a cheap and plentiful supply for the national workmen, and where the article is either peculiar to the country, or of peculiar quality there, the jealousy of enabling foreign workmen to rival those of the nation with its own materials, are the leading motives to this species of regulation. It ought not to be affirmed that it is in no instance proper; but is, certainly, one which ought to be adopted with great circumspection, and only in very plain cases. . . .

4. Pecuniary bounties.

This has been found one of the most efficacious means of encouraging manufactures, and is, in some views, the best. . . .

5. Premiums.

These are of a nature allied to bounties, though distinguishable from them in some important features.

Bounties are applicable to the whole quantity of an article produced, or manufactured, or exported, and involve a correspondent expense. . . .

6. The exemption of the materials of manufactures from duty.

The policy of that exemption, as a general rule, particularly in reference to new establishments, is obvious. It can hardly ever be advisable to add the obstructions of fiscal burthens to the difficulties which naturally embarrass a new manufacture; and where it is matured, and in condition to become an object of revenue, it is, generally speaking, better that the fabric, than the material, should be the subject of taxation. . . .

7. Drawbacks of the duties which are imposed on the materials of manufactures.

It has already been observed, as a general rule, that duties on those materials ought, with certain exceptions, to be forborne. Of these exceptions, three cases occur, which may serve as examples. One, where the material is itself an object of general or extensive consumption, and a fit and productive source of revenue. Another, where a manufacture of a simpler kind, the competition of which, with a like domestic article, is desired to be restrained, partakes of the nature of a raw material, from being capable, by a further process, to be converted into a manufacture of a different kind, the introduction or growth of which is desired to be encouraged. . . .

8. The encouragement of new inventions and discoveries at home, and of the introduction into the United States of such as may have been made in other countries; particularly those which relate to machinery.

This is among the most useful and unexceptionable of the aids which can be given to manufactures. The usual means of that encouragement are pecuniary rewards, and, for a time, exclusive privileges. The first must be employed according to the occasion and the utility of the invention or discovery. For the last, so far as respects "authors and inventors," provision has been made by law. . . .

9. Judicious regulations for the inspections of manufactured commodities.

This is not among the least important of the means by which the prosperity of manufactures may be promoted. It is, indeed, in many cases, one of the most essential. Contributing to prevent frauds upon consumers at home and exporters to foreign countries, to improve the quality and preserve the character of the national manufactures, it cannot fail to aid the expeditious and advantageous sale of them, and to serve as a guard against successful competition from other quarters. The reputation of the flour and lumber of some States, and of the potash of others, has been established by an attention to this point. And the like good name might be procured for those articles, wheresoever produced, by a judicious and uniform system of inspection throughout the ports of the United States. A like system might also be extended with advantage to other commodities.

10. The facilitating of pecuniary remittances from place to place.

. . . is a point of considerable moment to trade in general, and to manufacturers in particular, by rendering more easy the purchase of raw materials and provisions, and the payment for manufactured supplies. A general circulation of bank paper, which is to be expected from the institution lately established, will be a most valuable means to this end. . . .

11. The facilitating of the transportation of commodities.

Improvements favoring this object intimately concern all the domestic interests of a community; but they may, without impropriety, be mentioned as having an important relation to manufactures. There is, perhaps, scarcely anything which has been better calculated to assist the manufacturers of Great Britain than the melioration of the public roads of that kingdom, and the great progress which has been of late made in opening canals. Of the former, the United States stand much in need; for the latter, they present uncommon facilities.

The symptoms of attention to the improvement of inland navigation, which have lately appeared in some quarters, must fill with pleasure every breast warmed with a true zeal for the prosperity of the country. These examples, it is to be hoped, will stimulate the exertions of the government and citizens of every State. There can certainly be no object more worthy of the cares of the local administrations; and it were to be wished that there was no doubt of the power of the National Government to lend its direct aid on a comprehensive plan. This is one of those improvements which could be prosecuted with more efficacy by the whole than by any part or parts of the Union. There are cases in which the general interest will be in danger to be sacrificed to the collision of some supposed local interests. Jealousies, in matters of this kind, are as apt to exist as they are apt to be erroneous.

The Federalist Papers

The *Federalist Papers* was a series of eighty-five articles, the last of which appeared in May 1788, in which the Constitution was thoroughly discussed and generally supported. It remains to this day an outstanding commentary on the American system of government.

Alexander Hamilton conceived the idea that the Constitution should be explained to the American people. It is believed that he wrote fifty-nine or sixty of the articles, the remaining ones being written by John Jay and James Madison. The introduction to the *Federalist Papers*—written by Hamilton signed as "Publius" as were all of the articles—is a plea for ratification of the Constitution.*

After full experience of the insufficiency of the existing federal government, you are invited to deliberate upon a New Constitution for the United States of America. The subject speaks its own importance; comprehending in its consequences, nothing less than the existence of the UNION, the safety and welfare of the parts of which it is composed, the fate of an empire in many respects, the most interesting in the world. It has been frequently remarked, that it seems to have been reserved to the people of this country to decide, by their conduct and example, the important question, whether societies of men are really capable or not, of establishing good government from reflection and choice, or whether they are forever destined to depend, for their political constitutions, on accident and force. If there be any truth in the remark, the crisis at which we are arrived may, with propriety, be regarded as the period when that decision is to be made; and a wrong election of the part we shall act, may, in this view, deserve to be considered as the general misfortune of mankind.

This idea, by adding the inducements of philanthropy to those of patriotism, will heighten the solicitude which all considerate and good men must feel for the event. Happy will it be if our choice should be directed by a judicious estimate of our true interests, uninfluenced by considerations foreign to the public good. But this is more ardently to be wished for, than seriously to be expected. The plan offered to our deliberations, affects too many particular interests, innovates upon too many local institutions, not to involve in its discussion a variety of objects extraneous to its merits, and of views, passions and prejudices little favourable to the discovery of truth.

Among the most formidable of the obstacles which the new constitution will have to encounter, may readily be distinguished the obvious interest of a certain class of men in every state to resist all changes which may hazard a diminution of the power, emolument and consequence of the offices they hold under the state establishments . . . and the perverted ambition of another class of men, who will either hope to aggrandize themselves by the confusions of their country, or will flatter themselves with fairer prospects of elevation from the subdivision of the empire

*Introduction to THE FEDERALIST PAPERS by Alexander Hamilton, May, 1818.

into several partial confederacies, than from its union under one government.

It is not, however, my design to dwell upon observations of this nature. I am aware that it would be disingenuous to resolve indiscriminately the opposition of any set of men into interested or ambitious views, merely because their situations might subject them to suspicion. Candour will oblige us to admit, that even such men may be actuated by upright intentions; and it cannot be doubted, that much of the opposition, which has already shown itself, or that may hereafter make its appearance, will spring from sources blameless at least, if not respectable . . . the honest errors of minds led astray by preconceived jealousies and fears. So numerous indeed and so powerful are the causes which serve to give a false bias to the judgement, that we, upon many occasions, see wise and good men on the wrong as well as on the right side of questions, of the first magnitude to society. This circumstance, if duly attended to, would always furnish a lesson of moderation to those, who are engaged in any controversy, however well persuaded of being in the right. And a further reason for caution, in this respect, might be drawn from the reflection, that we are not always sure, that those who advocate the truth are actuated by purer principles than their antagonists. Ambition, avarice, personal animosity, party opposition, and many other motives, not more laudable than these, are apt to operate as well upon those who support, as upon those who oppose, the right side of a question. Were there not even these inducements to moderation, nothing could be more ill judged than that intolerant spirit, which has, at all times, characterized political parties. For, in politics as in religion, it is equally absurd to aim at making proselytes by fire and sword. Heresies in either can rarely be cured by persecution.

And yet, just as these sentiments must appear to candid men, we have already sufficient indications, that it will happen in this, as in all former cases of great national discussion. A torrent of angry and malignant passions will be let loose. To judge from the conduct of the opposite parties, we shall be led to conclude, that they will mutually hope to evince the justness of their opinions, and to increase the number of their converts, by the loudness of their declamations, and by the bitterness of their invectives. An enlightened zeal for the energy and efficiency of government, will be stigmatized as the offspring of a temper fond of power, and hostile to the principles of liberty. An over scrupulous jealousy of danger to the rights of the people, which is more commonly the fault of the head than of the heart, will be represented as mere pretense and artifice . . . the stale bait for popularity at the expense of public good. It will be forgotten, on the one hand, that jealousy is the usual concomitant of violent love, and that the noble enthusiasm of liberty is too apt to be infected with a spirit of narrow and illiberal distrust. On the other hand, it will be equally forgotten, that the vigour of government is essential to the security of liberty; that, in the contemplation of a sound and well informed judgment, their interests can never be separated; and that a dangerous ambition more often lurks behind the specious mask of zeal for the rights of the people, than under the forbidding appearances of zeal for the firmness and efficiency of government. History will teach us, that the former has been found a much more certain road to the introduction of despotism, than the latter, and that of those men who have overturned the liberties of republics, the greatest number have begun their career, by paying an obsequious court to the people . . . commencing demagogues, and ending tyrants.

In the course of the preceding observations it has been my aim, fellow citizens, to put you upon your guard against all attempts, from whatever quarter, to influence your decision in a matter of the utmost moment to your welfare, by any impressions, other than those which may result from the evidence of truth. You will, no doubt, at the same time, have collected from the general scope of them, that they proceed from a source not unfriendly to the new constitution. Yes, my countrymen, I own to you, that, after having given it an attentive consideration, I am clearly of opinion, it is your interest to adopt it. I am convinced, that this is the safest course for your liberty, your dignity, and your happiness. I affect not reserves, which I do not feel. I will not amuse you with an appearance of deliberation, when I have decided. I frankly acknowledge to you my convictions, and I will freely lay before you the reasons on which they are founded. The consciousness of good intentions disdains ambiguity. I shall not however multiply professions on this head. My motives must remain in the depository of my own breast: my arguments will be open to all, and may be judged of by all. They shall at least be offered in a spirit, which will not disgrace the cause of truth.

I propose, in a series of papers, to discuss the following interesting particulars. . . . *The utility of the UNION to your political prosperity.* . . . *The insufficiency of the present confederation to preserve that Union.* . . . *The necessity of a government at least equally energetic with the one proposed, to the attainment of this object.* . . . *The conformity of the proposed constitution to the true principles of republican government.* . . . *Its analogy to your own state constitution* . . . and lastly, *The additional security, which its adoption will afford to the preservation of that species of government, to liberty and to property.*

In the progress of this discussion, I shall endeavour to give a satisfactory answer to all the objections which shall have made their appearance, that may seem to have any claim to attention.

It may perhaps be thought superfluous to offer arguments to prove the utility of the UNION, a point, no doubt, deeply engraved on the hearts of the great body of the people in every state, and one which, it may be imagined, has no adversaries. But the fact is, that we already hear it whispered in the private circles of those who oppose the new constitution, that the Thirteen States are of too great extent for any general system, and that we must of necessity resort to separate confederacies of distinct portions of the whole. This doctrine will, in all probability, be gradually propagated, till it has votaries enough to countenance its open avowal. For nothing can be more evident, to those who are able to take an enlarged view of the subject, than the alternative of an adoption of the constitution, or a dismemberment of the Union. It may, therefore, be essential to examine particularly the advantages of that Union, the certain evils, and the probable dangers, to which every state will be exposed from its dissolution. This shall accordingly be done.

PUBLIUS.

Jefferson on Hamilton's Financial Policies

Thomas Jefferson was very much opposed to Hamilton's financial policies as well as his basic philosophy concerning the nature of the Union and the future of the United States. In the following personal letter to James Madison written in 1790, Jefferson expressed dissatisfaction with Hamilton's financial policies. He stated that the financial affairs of the United States should be "capable of being understood by common farmers."*

To James Madison

Monticello, March 6, 1790
Dear Sir: I do not at all wonder at the condition in which the finances of the United States are found. Hamilton's object from the beginning, was to throw

them into forms which should be utterly undecipherable. I ever said he did not understand their condition himself, nor was able to give a clear view of the excess of our debts beyond our credits, nor whether we were diminishing or increasing the debt. My own opinion was, that from the commencement of this Government to the time I ceased to attend to the subject, we had been increasing our debt about a million of dollars annually. If Mr. Gallatin would undertake to reduce this chaos to order, present us with a clear view of our finances, and put them into a form as simple as they will admit, he will merit immortal honor. The accounts of the United States ought to be, and may be made as simple as those of a common farmer, and capable of being understood by common farmers. . . .

The Constitutionality of a National Bank

In 1791, the major conflict between Jefferson and Hamilton on financial matters came to a head over the constitutionality of a national bank. Jefferson believed that the federal government had only the power specifically given to it in the Constitution. He felt that one could not broadly or loosely interpret the Constitution and thus the government could not use the "welfare" or "necessary and proper" clauses to justify the creation of a national bank. In short, Jefferson took the Constitution literally and Hamilton did not.*

February 15, 1791.
The bill for establishing a National Bank undertakes among other things:

1. To form the subscribers into a corporation.
2. To enable them in their corporate capacities to receive grants of land; and so far is against the laws of *Mortmain.*
3. To make alien subscribers capable of holding lands; and so far is against the laws of *alienage.*
4. To transmit these lands, on the death of a proprietor, to a certain line of successors; and so far changes the course of *Descents.*
5. To put the lands out of the reach of forfeiture or escheat; and so far is against the laws of *Forfeiture and Escheat.*
6. To transmit personal chattels to successors in a

*Private Letter to James Madison on Hamilton's Financial Policies by Thomas Jefferson in William Parker and Jonas Viles (eds.), LETTERS AND ADDRESSES OF THOMAS JEFFERSON, The National Jefferson Society, 1903.

*On the Constitutionality of a National Bank by Thomas Jefferson in William Parker and Jonas Viles (eds.), LETTERS AND ADDRESSES OF THOMAS JEFFERSON, The National Jefferson Society, 1903.

certain line; and so far is against the laws of *Distribution.*

7. To give them the sole and exclusive right of banking under the national authority; and so far is against the laws of *Monopoly.*

8. To communicate to them a power to make laws paramount to the laws of the States; for so they must be construed, to protect the institution from the control of the State legislatures; and so, probably, they will be construed.

I consider the foundation of the Constitution as laid on this ground: That "all powers not delegated to the United States, by the Constitution, nor prohibited by it to the States, are reserved to the States or to the people." (XIIth amendment.) To take a single step beyond the boundaries thus specially drawn around the powers of Congress, is to take possession of a boundless field of power, no longer susceptible of any definition.

The incorporation of a bank, and the powers assumed by this bill, have not, in my opinion, been delegated to the United States, by the Constitution.

I. They are not among the powers specially enumerated: for these are: 1st. A power to lay taxes for the purpose of paying the debts of the United States; but no debt is paid by this bill, nor any tax laid. . . .

2d. "To borrow money." But this bill neither borrows money nor insures the borrowing it. . . .

3d. To "regulate commerce with foreign nations, and among the States, and with the Indian tribes." To erect a bank and to regulate commerce, are very different acts. . . . Still less are these powers covered by any other of the special enumerations.

II. Nor are they within either of the general phrases, which are the two following:

1. To lay taxes to provide for the general welfare of the United States, that is to say, "to lay taxes for *the purpose* of providing for the general welfare." For the laying of taxes is the *power*, and the general welfare the *purpose* for which the power is to be exercised. They are not to lay taxes *ad libitum for any purpose they please*; but only *to pay the debts or provide for the welfare of the Union*. In like manner, they are not *to do anything they please* to provide for the general welfare, but only to *lay taxes* for that purpose. To consider the latter phrase, not as describing the purpose of the first, but as giving a distinct and independent power to do any act they please, which might be for the good of the Union, would render all the preceding and subsequent enumerations of power completely useless.

It would reduce the whole instrument to a single phrase, that of instituting a Congress with power to do whatever would be for the good of the United States; and, as they would be the sole judges of the good or evil, it would be also a power to do whatever evil they please.

It is an established rule of construction where a phrase will bear either of two meanings, to give it that which will allow some meaning to the other parts of the instrument, and not that which would render all the others useless. Certainly no such universal power was meant to be given them. It was intended to lace them up straitly within the enumerated powers, and those without which, as means, these powers could not be carried into effect. It is known that the very power now proposed *as a means* was rejected as *an end* by the Convention which formed the Constitution. A proposition was made to them to authorize Congress to open canals, and an amendatory one to empower them to incorporate. But the whole was rejected, and one of the reasons for rejection urged in debate was, that then they would have a power to erect a bank, which would render the great cities, where there were prejudices and jealousies on the subject, adverse to the reception of the Constitution.

2. The second general phrase is, "to make all laws *necessary* and proper for carrying into execution the enumerated powers." But they can all be carried into execution without a bank. A bank therefore is not *necessary*, and consequently not authorized by this phrase.

It has been urged that a bank will give great facility or convenience in the collection of taxes. Suppose this were true: yet the Constitution allows only the means which are "*necessary*," not those which are merely "convenient" for effecting the enumerated powers. If such a latitude of construction be allowed to this phrase as to give any non-enumerated power, it will go to every one, for there is not one which ingenuity may not torture into a *convenience* in some instance *or other*, to *some one* of so long a list of enumerated powers. It would swallow up all the delegated powers, and reduce the whole to one power, as before observed. Therefore it was that the Constitution restrained them to the *necessary* means, that is to say, to those means without which the grant of power would be nugatory. . . .

Can it be thought that the Constitution intended that for a shade or two of *convenience*, more or less, Congress should be authorized to break down the most ancient and fundamental laws of the several States; such as those against Mortmain, the laws of Alienage, the rules of descent, the acts of distribution, the laws of escheat and forfeiture, the laws of monopoly? Nothing but a necessity invincible by any other means, can justify such a prostitution of laws, which constitute the pillars of our whole system of jurisprudence. Will Congress be too straitlaced to carry the Constitution into honest effect, unless they may pass over the foundation-laws of the State government for the slightest convenience of theirs?

The negative of the President is the shield provided by the Constitution to protect against the invasions of the legislature: 1. The right of the Executive. 2. Of the Judiciary. 3. Of the States and State legislatures. The present is the case of a right remaining exclusively with the States, and consequently one of those intended by the Constitution to be placed under its protection.

It must be added, however, that unless the President's mind on a view of everything which is urged for and against this bill, is tolerably clear that it is unauthorized by the Constitution; if the pro and the con hang so even as to balance his judgment, a just respect for the wisdom of the legislature would naturally decide the balance in favor of their opinion. It is chiefly for cases where they are clearly misled by error, ambition, or interest, that the Constitution has placed a check in the negative of the President.

Washington's Farewell Address to the People of the United States

Washington's Farewell Address to the People of the United States was an attempt on the part of the first president to share with the American people of 1796 his wisdom, experience, and thoughts for the future. By retiring after eight years in the presidency, Washington established a tradition that no president should serve more than two terms. This tradition became law in 1951 when the Twenty-second Amendment to the Constitution was passed.

The reader should note Washington's references to the danger of political parties, sectionalism within the United States, an overgrown military establishment, a national debt, and permanent political alliances.*

Friends and Fellow Citizens:

The period for a new election of a citizen, to administer the executive government of the United States, being not far distant, and the time actually arrived when your thoughts must be employed in designating the person who is to be clothed with that important trust, it appears to me proper, especially as it may conduce to a more distinct expression of the public voice, that I should now apprise you of the resolution I have formed, to decline being considered among the number of those out of whom a choice is to be made.

While, then, every part of our country thus feels an immediate and particular interest in union, all the parts combined cannot fail to find in the united mass of means and efforts greater strength, greater resource, proportionally greater security from external danger, a less frequent interruption of their peace by foreign nations, and, what is of inestimable value, they must derive from union an exemption from those broils and wars between themselves, which so frequently afflict neighboring countries not tied together by the same governments, which their own rivalships alone would be sufficient to produce, but which opposite foreign alliances, attachments, and intrigues would stimulate and embitter. Hence, likewise, they will avoid the necessity of those overgrown military establishments which, under any form of government, are inauspicious to liberty, and which are to be regarded as particularly hostile to republican liberty.

I have already intimated to you the danger of parties in the State, with particular reference to the founding of them on geographical discrimination. Let me now take a more comprehensive view, and warn you in the most solemn manner against the baneful effects of the spirit of party, generally.

This spirit, unfortunately, is inseparable from our nature, having its root in the strongest passions of the human mind. It exists under different shapes in all governments, more or less stifled, controlled, or repressed; but in those of the popular form it is seen in its greatest rankness, and is truly their worst enemy.

The alternate domination of one faction over another, sharpened by the spirit of revenge, natural to party dissension, which in different ages and countries has perpetrated the most horrid enormities, is itself a frightful despotism. But this leads at length to a more formal and permanent despotism. The disorders and miseries which result, gradually incline the minds of men to seek security and repose in the absolute power of an individual; and sooner or later the chief of some prevailing faction, more able or more fortunate than his competitors, turns this disposition to the purposes of his own elevation, on the ruins of public liberty.

Without looking forward to an extremity of this kind (which nevertheless ought not to be entirely out of sight), the common and continued mischiefs of the

*George Washington, *Farewell Address to the People of the United States,* Riverside Press, 1913.

spirit of party are sufficient to make it the interest and duty of a wise people to discourage and restrain it.

It serves always to distract the public councils, and enfeeble the public administration. It agitates the community with ill-founded jealousies and false alarms; kindles the animosity of one part against another, foments occasionally riot and insurrection. It opens the doors to foreign influence and corruption, which find a facilitated access to the government itself through the channels of party passions. Thus the policy and the will of one country are subjected to the policy and will of another.

There is an opinion, that parties in free countries are useful checks upon the administration of the government, and serve to keep alive the spirit of liberty. This within certain limits is probably true, and in governments of a monarchical cast, patriotism may look with indulgence, if not with favor, upon the spirit of party. But in those of the popular character, in governments purely elective, it is a spirit not to be encouraged. From their natural tendency, it is certain there will always be enough of that spirit for every salutary purpose. And there being constant danger of excess, the effort ought to be, by force of public opinion to mitigate and assuage it. A fire not to be quenched, it demands a uniform vigilance to prevent its bursting into a flame, lest, instead of warming, it should consume.

It is substantially true that virtue or morality is a necessary spring of popular government. The rule, indeed, extends with more or less force to every species of free government. Who, that is a sincere friend to it, can look with indifference upon attempts to shake the foundation of the fabric?

Promote, then, as an object of primary importance, institutions for the general diffusion of knowledge. In proportion as the structure of a government gives force to public opinion, it is essential that public opinion should be enlightened.

As a very important source of strength and security, cherish public credit. One method of preserving it is, to use it as sparingly as possible; avoiding occasions of expense by cultivating peace, but remembering also that timely disbursements to prepare for danger frequently prevent much greater disbursements to repel it; avoiding likewise the accumulation of debt, not only by shunning occasions of expense, but by vigorous exertion in time of peace to discharge the debts, which unavoidable wars may have occasioned, not ungenerously throwing upon posterity the burden which we ourselves ought to bear. The execution of these maxims belongs to your representatives, but it is necessary that public opinion should co-operate. To facilitate to them the performance of their duty it is essential that you should practically bear in mind, that towards the payment of debts there must be revenue; that to have revenue there must be taxes; that no taxes can be devised which are not more or less inconvenient and unpleasant; that the intrinsic embarrassment, inseparable from the selection of the proper objects (which is always a choice of difficulties), ought to be a decisive motive for a candid construction of the conduct of the government in making it, and for a spirit of acquiescence in the measures for obtaining revenue which the public exigencies may at any time dictate.

Observe good faith and justice towards all nations; cultivate peace and harmony with all. Religion and morality enjoin this conduct; and can it be, that good policy does not equally enjoin it? It will be worthy of a free, enlightened, and at no distant period a great nation, to give to mankind the magnanimous and too novel example of a people always guided by an exalted justice and benevolence. Who can doubt that in the course of time and things, the fruits of such a plan would richly repay any temporary advantages, which might be lost by a steady adherence to it? Can it be that Providence has not connected the permanent felicity of a nation with its virtue? The experiment, at least, is recommended by every sentiment which ennobles human nature. Alas! is it rendered impossible by its vices?

In the execution of such a plan, nothing is more essential than that permanent, inveterate antipathies against particular nations, and passionate attachments for others, should be excluded; and that, in place of them, just and amicable feelings towards all should be cultivated. The nation which indulges towards another an habitual hatred, or an habitual fondness, is in some degree a slave. It is a slave to its animosity or to its affection, either of which is sufficient to lead it astray from its duty and its interest. Antipathy in one nation against another disposes each more readily to offer insult and injury, to lay hold of slight causes of umbrage, and to be haughty and intractable when accidental or trifling occasions of dispute occur. Hence, frequent collisions, obstinate, envenomed, and bloody contests. The nation, prompted by ill-will and resentment, sometimes impels to war the government, contrary to the best calculations of policy. The government sometimes participates in the national propensity, and adopts through passion what reason would reject; at other times, it makes the animosity of the nation subservient to projects of hostility instigated by pride, ambition, and other sinister and pernicious motives. The peace often, sometimes perhaps the liberty, of nations has been the victim.

So likewise, a passionate attachment of one nation for another produces a variety of evils. Sympathy for the favorite nation, facilitating the illusion of an imaginary common interest in cases where no real common interest exists, and infusing into one the enmities of the other, betrays the former into a participation in the quarrels and wars of the latter, without adequate inducement or justification. It leads also to concessions to the favorite nation of privileges denied to others, which is apt doubly to injure the nation making the concessions, by unnecessarily parting with what ought to have been retained, and by exciting jealousy, ill-will, and a disposition to retaliate, in the parties from whom equal privileges are withheld. And it gives to ambitious, corrupted, or deluded citizens (who devote themselves to the favorite nation), facility to betray or sacrifice the interests of their own country, without odium, sometimes even with popularity; gilding with the appearances of a virtuous sense of obligation, a commendable deference for public opinion, or a laudable zeal for public good, the base or foolish compliances of ambition, corruption, or infatuation.

As avenues to foreign influence in innumerable ways such attachments are particularly alarming to the truly enlightened and independent patriot. How many opportunities do they afford to tamper with domestic factions, to practise the arts of seduction, to mislead public opinion, to influence or awe the public councils! Such an attachment of a small or weak, towards a great and powerful nation, dooms the former to be the satellite of the latter.

Against the insidious wiles of foreign influence (I conjure you to believe me, fellow-citizens), the jealousy of a free people ought to be constantly awake, since history and experience prove that foreign influence is one of the most baneful foes of republican government. But that jealousy, to be useful, must be impartial; else it becomes the instrument of the very influence to be avoided, instead of a defence against it. Excessive partiality for one foreign nation, and excessive dislike of another, cause those whom they actuate to see danger only on one side, and serve to veil and even second the arts of influence on the other. Real patriots who may resist the intrigues of the favorite, are liable to become suspected and odious; while its tools and dupes usurp the applause and confidence of the people, to surrender their interests.

The great rule of conduct for us, in regard to foreign nations, is, in extending our commercial relations, to have with them as little political connection as possible. So far as we have already formed engagements, let them be fulfilled with perfect good faith. Here let us stop.

Europe has a set of primary interests, which to us have none, or a very remote relation. Hence she must be engaged in frequent controversies, the causes of which are essentially foreign to our concerns. Hence, therefore, it must be unwise in us to implicate ourselves, by artificial ties, in the ordinary vicissitudes of her politics, or the ordinary combinations and collisions of her friendships or enmities.

Our detached and distant situation invites and enables us to pursue a different course. If we remain one people, under an efficient government, the period is not far off when we may defy material injury from external annoyance; when we may take such an attitude as will cause the neutrality, we may at any time resolve upon, to be scrupulously respected; when belligerent nations, under the impossibility of making acquisitions upon us, will not lightly hazard the giving us provocation; when we may choose peace or war, as our interest, guided by justice, shall counsel.

Why forego the advantages of so peculiar a situation? Why quit our own to stand upon foreign ground? Why, by interweaving our destiny with that of any part of Europe, entangle our peace and prosperity in the toils of European ambition, rivalship, interest, humor, or caprice?

It is our true policy to steer clear of permanent alliances with any portion of the foreign world; so far, I mean, as we are now at liberty to do it; for let me not be understood as capable of patronizing infidelity to existing engagements. I hold the maxim no less applicable to public than to private affairs, that honesty is always the best policy. I repeat it, therefore, let those engagements be observed in their genuine sense. But, in my opinion, it is unnecessary and would be unwise to extend them.

AGE OF JEFFERSON AND JACKSON

"Jefferson and Liberty"

The election of 1800 was the first victory of the Democratic-Republican party, led by Thomas Jefferson. Opposition to the Federalist party had grown especially strong after passage of the Alien and Sedition Acts. The Jeffersonian party feared being entangled in Europe's wars and dreamed of a future free from war and oppression. Their campaign song was "Jefferson and Liberty.*

The_ gloom - y night_ be - fore us flies, The

reign of ter - ror now_ is o'er;Its gags, in-quis-i-

tors and spies, Its herds of Har-pies are no more.

CHORUS

Re - joice, Co - lum - bia's sons, re-joice; To

ty-rants nev - er bend the knee;But join with heart, and

soul and voice, For Jef - fer-son_ and lib - er - ty.

No lordling here with gorging jaws
Shall wring from industry the food,
Nor fiery bigot's holy laws
Lay waste our fields and streets in blood!
Chorus

Here strangers from a thousand shores
Compelled by tyranny to roam,
Shall find, amidst abundant stores
A nobler and a happier home.
Chorus

Here Art shall lift her laurel'd head,
Wealth, Industry, and Peace divine;
And where dark, pathless forests spread,
Rich fields and lofty cities shine.
Chorus

*From THE BALLAD OF AMERICA: THE HISTORY OF THE UNITED STATES IN SONG AND STORY by John Anthony Scott. Copyright © 1966 by Bantam Books, Inc.

"Sold Off to Georgy"

"Sold Off to Georgy" was first published in George Tucker's book *The Valley of the Shenandoah* in 1824. Tucker, a novelist who lived in Virginia, had heard the song sung by Negro slaves. The opening of new plantation lands in the South after the War of 1812 led to a greater demand for slaves. This song expresses the anguish of a slave being separated from family and friends as he is sold and sent from Virginia to Georgia.*

Fare - well, fel - low ser - vants, O -
ho! O - ho! I'm gwine 'way to leave you, O -
ho! O - ho! I'm gwine to leave de ole
coun - ty, O - ho! O - ho! I'm
sold off to Geor - gy, O - ho! O - ho!

Farewell, ole plantation,
Oho! Oho!
Farewell, de ole quarter,
Oho! Oho!
An' daddy, an' mammy,
Oho! Oho!
An' massa an' missus,
Oho! Oho!

My dear wife and one child,
Oho! Oho!
My poor heart is breaking,
Oho! Oho!
No more shall I see you,
Oho! Oho!
Oh, no more for ever,
Oho! Oho!

*From THE BALLAD OF AMERICA: THE HISTORY OF THE UNITED STATES IN SONG AND STORY by John Anthony Scott. Copyright © 1966 by Bantam Books, Inc.

Jefferson on Slavery

Thomas Jefferson's feelings toward slavery can be observed in much of his writing concerning politics, morality, and society in general. In the following excerpt from *Notes on Virginia* (1782), Jefferson points out that emancipation is inevitable because the Almighty is just and "his justice cannot sleep forever."*

There must doubtless be an unhappy influence on the manners of our people produced by the existence of slavery among us. The whole commerce between master and slave is a perpetual exercise of the most boisterous passions, the most unremitting despotism on the one part, and degrading submissions on the other. Our children see this, and learn to imitate it; for man is an imitative animal. This quality is the germ of all education in him. From his cradle to his grave he is learning to do what he sees others do. If a parent could find no motive either in his philanthropy or his self-love, for restraining the intemperance of passion toward his slave, it should always be a sufficient one that his child is present. But generally it is not sufficient. The parent storms, the child looks on, catches the lineaments of wrath, puts on the same airs in the circle of smaller slaves, gives a loose to the worst of passions, and thus nursed, educated, and daily exercised in tyranny, cannot but be stamped by it with odious peculiarities. The man must be a prodigy who can retain his manners and morals undepraved by such circumstances. And with what execration should the statesman be loaded, who, permitting one-half the citizens thus to trample on the rights of the other, transforms those into despots, and these into enemies, destroys the morals of the one part, and the *amor patriae* of the other. For if a slave can have a country in this world, it must be any other in preference to that in which he is born to live and labor for another; in which he must lock up the faculties of his nature, contribute as far as depends on his individual endeavors to the evanishment of the human race, or entail his own miserable condition on the endless generations proceeding from him. With the morals of the people, their industry also is destroyed. For in a warm climate, no man will labor for himself who can make another labor for him. This is so true, that of the proprietors of slaves a very small proportion indeed are ever seen to labor. And can the liberties of a nation be thought secure when we have removed their only firm basis, a conviction in the minds of the people that these liberties are of the gift of God? That they are not to be violated but with His wrath? Indeed, I tremble for my country when I reflect that God is just; that his justice cannot sleep forever; that considering numbers, nature and natural means only, a revolution of the wheel of fortune, an exchange of situation is among possible events; that it may become probable by supernatural interference! The Almighty has no attribute which can take side with us in such a contest. But it is impossible to be temperate and to pursue this subject through the various considerations of policy, of morals, of history natural and civil. We must be contented to hope they will force their way into every one's mind. I think a change already perceptible, since the origin of the present revolution. The spirit of the master is abatting, that of the slave rising from the dust, his condition mollifying, the way I hope preparing, under the auspices of heaven, for a total emancipation, and that this is disposed, in the order of events, to be with the consent of the masters, rather than by their extirpation.

On the Constitutionality of the Louisiana Purchase

The purchase of the Louisiana Territory in 1803 was the largest land purchase in American history, rivaled only by that of Alaska in 1867. The purchase was interesting from many points of view. The United States bought the land from France, but the sale violated certain agreements between France and Spain. The boundaries of the territory were not clear as they were tied up in various national claims. It could also be argued that Jefferson's purchase of the land was unconstitutional which is particularly interesting in the light of Jefferson's earlier strict interpretation of the Constitution in relation to the National Bank.

In the following letter to Wilson C. Nicholas in 1803, Jefferson tries to justify his action, while retaining his basic philosophy toward the Constitution.*

*Thomas Jefferson, *Notes on Virginia* in William Parker and Jonas Viles (eds.), LETTERS AND ADDRESSES OF THOMAS JEFFERSON, The National Jefferson Society, 1903.

*Letter to Wilson C. Nicholas from Thomas Jefferson in William Parker and Jonas Viles (eds.), LETTERS AND ADDRESSES OF THOMAS JEFFERSON, The National Jefferson Society, 1903.

To Wilson C. Nicholas

Monticello, September 7, 1803.

Dear Sir: I inclose you a letter from Monroe on the subject of the late treaty. You will observe a hint in it, to do without delay what we are bound to do. There is reason, in the opinion of our ministers, to believe, that if the thing were to do over again, it could not be obtained, and that if we give the least opening they will declare the treaty void. A warning amounting to that has been given to them, and an unusual kind of letter written by their minister to our Secretary of State, direct. Whatever Congress shall think it necessary to do, should be done with as little debate as possible, and particularly so far as respects the constitutional difficulty. I am aware of the force of the observations you make on the power given by the Constitution to Congress, to admit new States into the Union, without restraining the subject to the territory then constituting the United States. But when I consider that the limits of the United States are precisely fixed by the treaty of 1783, that the Constitution expressly declares itself to be made for the United States, I cannot help believing the intention was not to permit Congress to admit into the Union new States, which should be formed out of the territory for which, and under whose authority alone, they were then acting. I do not believe it was meant that they might receive England, Ireland, Holland, etc., into it, which would be the case on your construction. When an instrument admits two constructions, the one safe, the other dangerous, the one precise, the other indefinite, I prefer that which is safe and precise. I had rather ask an enlargement of power from the nation, where it is found necessary, than to assume it by a construction which would make our powers boundless. Our peculiar security is in the possession of a written Constitution. Let us not make it a blank paper by construction. I say the same as to the opinion of those who consider the grant of the treaty-making power as boundless. If it is, then we have no Constitution. If it has bounds, they can be no others than the definitions of the powers which that instrument gives. It specifies and delineates the operations permitted to the federal government, and gives all the powers necessary to carry these into execution. Whatever of these enumerated objects is proper for a law, Congress may make the law; whatever is proper to be executed by way of a treaty, the President and Senate may enter into the treaty; whatever is to be done by a judicial sentence, the judges may pass the sentence. Nothing is more likely than that their enumeration of powers is defective. This is the ordinary case of all human works. Let us go on

then perfecting it, by adding, by way of amendment to the Constitution, those powers which time and trial show are still wanting. But it has been taken too much for granted, that by this rigorous construction the treaty power would be reduced to nothing. I had occasion once to examine its effect on the French treaty, made by the old Congress, and found that out of thirty odd articles which that contained, there were one, two, or three only which could not now be stipulated under our present Constitution. I confess, then, I think it important, in the present case, to set an example against broad construction, by appealing for new power to the people. If, however, our friends shall think differently, certainly I shall acquiesce with satisfaction; confiding, that the good sense of our country will correct the evil of construction when it shall produce ill effects.

The Lewis and Clark Expedition

President Jefferson wanted to know more about the vast Louisiana territory, which he had just purchased. He wanted information concerning its geography, natural resources, climate, and inhabitants. Therefore, Jefferson engaged the services of Captain Meriwether Lewis as leader of an expedition and William Clark, brother of the well-known general George Rogers Clark, as Lewis's assistant, to travel into the territory and gather such information.

The following extract is taken from the journals of Lewis and Clark and was written by Clark in 1806 toward the end of the expedition in what is now South Dakota.*

Saturday 30th of August 1806. . . . I took 3 hunters and walked on the N. E. Shore with a view to kill some fat meet. we had not proceeded far before Saw a large plumb orchd. of the most delicious plumbs, out of this orchard 2 large Buck Elks ran the hunters killed them. I stoped the canoes and brought in the flesh which was fat and fine. here the party collected as many plumbs as they could eate and Several pecks of which they put by &c. after a delay of nearly 2 hours we again proceeded on downwards, I saw Several men on horse-

*From THE JOURNALS OF LEWIS AND CLARK. Copyright, 1953, by Bernard DeVoto. Reprinted by permission of the publisher, Houghton Mifflin Company.

back which with the help of a spie glass I found to be Indians on the high hills to the N. E. we landed on the S. W. side and I sent out two men to a village of Barking Squirels to kill some of those animals imedeatily after landing about 20 indians was discovered on an eminance a little above us on the opposite Side. one of those men I took to be a french man from his [having] a blanket capoe & a handkerchief around his head. imediately after 80 or 90 Indian men all armed with fusees & Bows & arrows came out of a wood on the opposite bank about ¼ of a mile below us. they fired of[f] their guns as a Salute we returned the Salute with 2 rounds. we were at a loss to deturmin of what nation those indians were. from their hostile appearance we were apprehensive they were Tetons, but from the country through which they roved we were willing to believe them either the Yanktons, Pon[c]ars or Mahars either of which nations are well disposed towards the white people. I deturmined to find out who they were without running any risque of the party and the indians, and therefore took three french men who could Speak the Mahar Pania and some Seeoux and in a Small canoe I went over to a Sand bar which extended Sufficiently near the opposite shore to converse.

imedeately after I set out 3 young men set out from the opposite Side and swam next me on the Sand bar. I derected the men to Speak to them in the Pania and Mahar Languages first neither of which they could understand I then derected the man who could speak a fiew words of Seioux to inquire what nation or tribe they belong to they informed me that they were Tetons and their chief was the black buffalow this chief I knew very well to be the one we had seen with his band at Teton river which band had attempted to detain us in the fall of 1804 as we assended this river and with whome we wer near comeing to blows. I told those Indians that they had been deef to our councils and ill treated us as we assended this river two years past, that they had abused all the whites who had visited them since. I believed them to be bad people & should not suffer them to cross to the Side on which the party lay, and directed them to return with their band to their camp, that if any of them come near our camp we Should kill them certainly. I lef[t] them on the bear [bar] and returned to th[e] party and examined the arms &c those indians seeing some corn in the canoe requested some of it which I refused being deturmined to have nothing to do with those people.

Several others swam across one of which understood pania, and as our pania interpreter was a very good one we had it in our power to inform what we wished. I told this man to inform his nation that we had not forgot their treatment to us as we passed up this river &c. that they had treated all the white people who had visited them very badly; robed them of their goods, and had wounded one man whom I had Seen. we viewed them as bad people and no more traders would be Suffered to come to them, and whenever the white people wished to visit the nations above they would come sufficiently Strong to whip any vilenous party who dare to oppose them and words to the same purpote. I also told them that I was informed that a part of all their bands were going to war against the Mandans &c, and that they would be well whiped as the Mandans & Minitarres &[c] had a plenty of Guns Powder and ball, and we had given them a cannon to defend themselves. and derected them to return from the Sand bar and inform their chiefs what we had said to them, and to keep away from the river or we Should kill every one of them &c. &c. those fellows requested to be allowed to come across and make cumerads which we positively refused and I directed them to return imediately which they did and after they had informed the Chiefs &c. as I suppose what we had said to them, they all set out on their return to their camps back of a high hill. 7 of them halted on the top of the hill and blackguarded us, told us to come across and they would kill us all &c of which we took no notice.

we all this time were extreamly anxious for the arival of the 2 fields & Shannon whome we had left behind, and were some what consd. as to their Safty to our great joy those men hove in Sight at 6 P. M. Jo Fields had killed 3 black tail or mule deer. we then Set out, as I wished to see what those Indians on the hill would act, we steared across near the opposit Shore, this notion put them [in] some agitation as to our intentions, some set out on the direction towards their Camps others walked about on the top of the hill and one man walked down the hill to meet us and invited us to land to which invitation I paid no kind of attention. this man I knew to be the one who had in the fall 1804 accompanied us 2 days and is said to be the friend to the white people. after we passd him he returned on the top of the hill and gave 3 strokes with the gun *(on the earth—this is swearing by the earth)* he had in his hand this I am informed is a great oath among the indians.

Anglo-American Relations and the Impending War of 1812

Thomas Jefferson left the White House in March 1809 after serving two terms as president. As can be observed in the following letter to an old English friend, dated April 25, 1812, Jefferson continued an active interest in political affairs. In this letter, the former president laments the drift of the United States and Britain toward war. He points out why he dislikes the foreign policies of both Britain and France and why he believes that "the object of England, long obvious, is to claim the ocean as her domain, and to exact transit duties from every vessel traversing it."*

To James Maury

Monticello, April 25, 1812.

My dear and ancient Friend and Classmate: Often has my heart smote me for delaying acknowledgments to you, receiving, as I do, such frequent proofs of your kind recollection in the transmission of papers to me. But instead of acting on the good old maxim of not putting off to to-morrow what we can do to-day, we are too apt to reverse it, and not to do to-day what we can put off to to-morrow. But this duty can be no longer put off. To-day we are at peace; to-morrow, war. The curtain of separation is drawing between us, and probably will not be withdrawn till one, if not both of us, will be at rest with our fathers. Let me now, then, while I may, renew to you the declarations of my warm attachment, which in no period of life has ever been weakened, and seems to become stronger as the remaining objects of our youthful affections are fewer.

Our two countries are to be at war, but not you and I. And why should our two countries be at war, when by peace we can be so much more useful to one another? Surely the world will acquit our Government from having sought it. Never before has there been an instance of a nation's bearing so much as we have borne. Two items alone in our catalogue of wrongs will forever acquit us of being the aggressors: the impressment of our seamen, and the excluding us from the ocean. The first foundations of the social compact would be broken up, were we definitively to refuse to its members the protection of their persons and property, while in their lawful pursuits. I think the war will not be short, because the object of England, long obvious, is to claim the ocean as her domain, and to exact transit duties from every vessel

*Personal Letter to an Old English Friend Concerning Anglo-American Relations and the Impending War of 1812 by Thomas Jefferson in William Parker and Jonas Viles (eds.), LETTERS AND ADDRESSES OF THOMAS JEFFERSON, The National Jefferson Society, 1903.

traversing it. This is the sum of her orders of council, which were only a step in this bold experiment, never meant to be retracted if it could be permanently maintained. And this object must continue her in war with all the world. To this I see no termination, until her exaggerated efforts, so much beyond her natural strength and resources, shall have exhausted her to bankruptcy. The approach of this crisis is, I think, visible in the departure of her precious metals, and depreciation of her paper medium. We, who have gone through that operation, know its symptoms, its course, and consequences. In England they will be more serious than elsewhere, because half the wealth of her people is now in that medium, the private revenue of her money-holders, or rather of her paper-holders, being, I believe, greater than that of her land-holders. Such a proportion of property, imaginary and baseless as it is, cannot be reduced to vapor but with great explosion. She will rise out of its ruins, however, because her lands, her houses, her arts will remain, and the greater part of her men. And these will give her again that place among nations which is proportioned to her natural means, and which we all wish her to hold. We believe that the just standing of all nations is the health and security of all. We consider the overwhelming power of England on the ocean, and of France on the land, as destructive of the prosperity and happiness of the world, and wish both to be reduced only to the necessity of observing moral duties. We believe no more in Bonaparte's fighting merely for the liberty of the seas, than in Great Britain's fighting for the liberties of mankind. The object of both is the same, to draw to themselves the power, the wealth, and the resources of other nations. We resist the enterprises of England first, because they first come vitally home to us. And our feelings repel the logic of bearing the lash of George the III. for fear of that of Bonaparte at some future day. When the wrongs of France shall reach us with equal effect, we shall resist them also. But one at a time is enough; and having offered a choice to the champions, England first takes up the gauntlet.

The English newspapers suppose me the personal enemy of their nation. I am not so. I am an enemy to its injuries, as I am to those of France. If I could permit myself to have national partialities, and if the conduct of England would have permitted them to be directed toward her, they would have been so. I thought that in the administration of Mr. Addington, I discovered some dispositions toward justice, and even friendship and respect for us, and began to pave the way for cherishing these dispositions, and improving them into ties of mutual goodwill. But we had then a federal minister there, whose dispositions to believe himself, and to inspire others with a belief, in our sincerity, his subsequent conduct has brought into doubt; and poor Merry, the English minister here, had learned nothing of diplomacy but its suspicions, without head enough to distinguish when they were misplaced. Mr. Addington and Mr. Fox passed away too soon to avail the two countries of their dispositions. Had I been personally hostile to England, and biassed in favor of either the character or views of her great antagonist, the affair of the Chesapeake put war into my hand. I had only to open it and let havoc loose. But if ever I was gratified with the possession of power, and of the confidence of those who had intrusted me with it, it was on that occasion when I was enabled to use both for the prevention of war, toward which the torrent of passion here was directed almost irresistibly, and when not another person in the United States, less supported by authority and favor, could have resisted it. And now that a definitive adherence to her impressments and orders of council renders war no longer avoidable, my earnest prayer is that our Government may enter into no compact of common cause with the other belligerents, but keep us free to make a separate peace, whenever England will separately give us peace and future security. But Lord Liverpool is our witness that this can never be but by her removal from our neighborhood.

I have thus, for a moment, taken a range into the field of politics, to possess you with the view we take of things here. But in the scenes which are to ensue I am to be but a spectator. I have withdrawn myself from all political intermeddlings, to indulge the evening of my life with what have been the passions of every portion of it, books, science, my farms, my family and friends. To these every hour of the day is now devoted. I retain a good activity of mind, not quite as much of body, but uninterrupted health. Still the hand of age is upon me. All my old friends are nearly gone. Of those in my neighborhood, Mr. Divers and Mr. Lindsay alone remain. If you could make it a *partie quarrée,* it would be a comfort indeed. We would beguile our lingering hours with talking over our youthful exploits, our hunts on Peter's mountain, with a long train of *et cetera,* in addition, and feel, by recollection, at least, a momentary flash of youth. Reviewing the course of a long and sufficiently successful life, I find in no portion of it happier moments than those were. I think the old hulk in which you are, is near her wreck, and that, like a prudent rat, you should escape in time. However, here, there, and everywhere, in peace or in war, you will have my sincere affections and prayers for your life, health, and happiness.

The *Constitution* and the *Guerrière*

One of the most colorful naval battles in American history was between two men-of-war in the War of 1812—the *Constitution* and the *Guerrière.* The account given here depicts how the U.S.S. *Constitution*—which is still commissioned in the United States Navy and is on display in Boston Harbor—defeated the British vessel on August 19, 1812.*

Up to the affair of the *Constitution* and the *Guerrière,* in 1812, the British had not fairly tested in battle the seamanship or naval metal of the Americans. With the exceptions of the actions between the *Bonhomme Richard* and the *Serapis,* the *Ranger* and *Drake,* and the *Yarmouth* and *Randolph,* the war of '76 was a repelled invasion.

The twenty-four hours of the 19th of August, 1812, began with light breezes that freshened as the morning wore on. The *Constitution* was slipping southward through the long rolling seas.

A month before this date, under the command of Commodore Hull, she had made her wonderful escape from Broke's squadron after a chase of over sixty hours.

Her cruise since she had left Boston, two weeks before, had been uneventful. Vainly had she sought from Cape Sable to the region of Halifax, from Nova Scotia to the Gulf of St. Lawrence, for any sign of a foe worthy her metal. It was getting on towards two o'clock; her men had finished their mid-day meal, the afternoon drills had not begun and an observation showed the ship to be in latitude 41° 40′ and longitude 55° 48′. Suddenly "Sail ho!" from the masthead stirred the groups on the forecastle, and caused the officer pacing the weather side of the quarterdeck to stop suddenly and raise his head.

"Where away?" he shouted to the voice far up above the booming sails.

Almost before he could get the answer the stranger's top-sails were visible from the lower rigging, into which the midshipmen and idlers had scrambled, and a few moments later they could be seen from the upper deck. The vessel was too far off to show her character, but bore E.S.E., a faint dot against the horizon.

Hull came immediately from his cabin. He was a large, fat man, whose excitable temperament was held in strong control. His eye gleamed when he saw the distant speck of white. Immediately the *Constitu-*

*From James Barnes, NAVAL ACTIONS OF THE WAR OF 1812, Harper & Brothers, 1896.

tion's course was altered, and with her light sails set she was running free, with kites all drawing, and the chase looming clearer and clearer each anxious minute of the time. At three o'clock it was plainly seen that she was a large ship, on the starboard tack, close-hauled on the wind, and under easy sail. In half an hour her ports could be descried through the glass, and loud murmurs of satisfaction ran through the ship's company. The officers smiled congratulations at one another, and Hull's broad face shone with his suppressed emotion. In the official account Hull speaks of the conduct of his crew before the fight in the following words: "It gives me great pleasure to say that from the smallest boy in the ship to the oldest seaman not a look of fear was seen. They went into action giving three cheers, and requesting to be laid close to the enemy." The *Constitution* gained on the stranger, who held her course, as if entirely oblivious of her pursuer's presence.

When within three miles, and to leeward, Hull shortened sail and cleared the decks; the drum beat to quarters, and the men sprang to their stations. No crew was ever better prepared to do battle for any cause or country. Although few of the men had been in action before, they had been drilled until they had the handling of the clumsy iron guns down to the point of excellence. They had been taught to fire on the falling of a sea, and to hull their opponent, if possible, at every shot. They loved and trusted their commander, were proud of their ship, and burned to avenge the wrongs to which many had been subjected, for the merchant service had furnished almost half their number.

As soon as Hull took in his sail the stranger backed her main-topsail yard, and slowly came up into the wind. Then it could be seen that *her* men were all at quarters also. Hull raised his flag. Immediately in response up went to every mast-head of the waiting ship the red cross of old England. It was growing late in the afternoon, the breeze had freshened, and the white-caps had begun to jump on every side. The crew of the *Constitution* broke into three ringing cheers as their grand old craft bore down upon the enemy. When almost within range the English let go her broadside, filled away, wore ship, and fired her other broadside on the other tack. The shot fell short, and the *Constitution* reserved her fire. For three-quarters of an hour the two yawed about and manoeuvred, trying to rake and to avoid being raked in turn. Occasionally the *Constitution* fired a gun; her men were in a fever of impatience.

At six in the evening the enemy, seeing all attempts to outsail her antagonist were in vain, showed a brave indication of wishing to close and fight. Nearer the two approached, the American in silence.

"Shall I fire?" inquired Lieutenant Morris, Hull's second in command.

"Not yet," replied Hull, quietly.

The bows of the *Constitution* began to double the quarter of the enemy. The latter's shot began to start the sharp white splinters flying about the *Constitution's* decks.

"Shall I fire?" again asked Lieutenant Morris.

"Not yet, sir," was Hull's answer, spoken almost beneath his breath. Suddenly he bent forward. "Now, boys," he shouted, loudly, so that his voice rang above the enemy's shots and the roaring of the seas under the quarter, "pour it into them!" It was at this point, so the story goes, that Hull, crouching in his excitement, split his tight knee-breeches from waist-band to buckle.

The *Constitution's* guns were double-shotted with round and grape. The broadside was as one single explosion, and the destruction was terrific. The enemy's decks were flooded, and the blood ran out of the scuppers—her cockpit filled with the wounded. For a few minutes, shrouded in smoke, they fought at the distance of a half pistol-shot, but in that short space of time the Englishman was literally torn to pieces in hull, spars, sails, and rigging.

As her mizzenmast gave way the Englishman brought up into the wind, and the *Constitution* forged slowly ahead, fired again, luffed short around the other's bows, and, owing to the heavy sea, fell foul of her antagonist, with her bowsprit across her larboard quarter. While in this position Hull's cabin was set on fire by the enemy's forward battery, and part of the crew were called away from the guns to extinguish the threatening blaze.

Now both sides tried to board. It was the old style of fighting for the British tars, and they bravely swarmed on deck at the call, "Boarders away!" and the shrill piping along the 'tween-decks. The Americans were preparing for the same attempt, and three of their officers who mounted the taffrail were shot by the muskets of the English. Brave Lieutenant Bush, of the marines, fell dead with a bullet in his brain.

The swaying and grinding of the huge ships against each other made boarding impossible, and it was at this anxious moment that the sails of the *Constitution* filled; she fell off and shot ahead. Hardly was she clear when the foremast of the enemy fell, carrying with it the wounded mainmast, and leaving the proud vessel of a few hours before a helpless wreck, "rolling like a log in the trough of the sea, entirely at the mercy of the billows."

It was now nearly seven o'clock. The sky had clouded over, the wind was freshening, and the sea was growing heavy. Hull drew off for repairs, rove new rigging, secured his masts, and, wearing ship, again approached, ready to pour in a final broadside. It was not needed. Before the *Constitution* could fire, the flag which had been flying at the stump of the enemy's mizzenmast was struck. The fight was over.

A boat was lowered from the *Constitution*, and Lieutenant Read, the third officer, rowing to the prize, inquired, with "Captain Hull's compliments," if she had struck her flag. He was answered by Captain Dacres—who must have possessed a sense of humor—that, for very obvious reasons, she certainly had done so.

To quote a few words from Hull's account of the affair—he says: "After informing that so fine a ship as the *Guerrière*, commanded by an able and experienced officer, had been totally dismasted and otherwise cut to pieces, so as to make her not worth towing into port, in the short space of thirty minutes (actual fighting time), you can have no doubt of the gallantry and good conduct of the officers and ship's company I have the honor to command."

In the *Constitution* seven were killed and seven wounded. In the *Guerrière*, fifteen killed, sixty-two wounded—including several officers and the captain, who was wounded slightly; twenty-four were missing. . . .

The Battle of New Orleans

The reputation of General Andrew Jackson was greatly increased following the victory of his forces in the Battle of New Orleans, January 1815. A truce ending the War of 1812 had been arranged two weeks before this battle, but neither side at New Orleans knew this. Many of the British soldiers who fought in the battle had gained a great deal of military experience in Europe against the armies of Napoleon. In contrast, Jackson's forces were a group of irregular soldiers from Tennessee, Louisiana, and Kentucky.*

At one o'clock on the morning of this memorable day, on a couch in a room of the Macarty mansion-house, General Jackson lay asleep, in his worn uniform. Several of his aids slept upon the floor in the same apartment, all equipped for the field, except that their sword-belts were unbuckled and their swords and pistols laid aside. A sentinel paced the adjacent passage. Sentinels moved noiselessly about the building, which loomed up large, dim and silent in the foggy night, among the darkening trees. Most of those who slept at all that night were still asleep and there was as yet little stir in either camp to disturb their slumbers. . . .

"It was astonishing to see how many men—private soldiers—the General could call by name. He knew every Tennesseean and at least half the Kentuckians. His manner with them was easy—a modern general would call it familiar. Still he was dignified and they all seemed to understand him.

* * *

"General Jackson, Carroll and Adair and Major Latour, Mr. Livingston and I got up on the parapet. In a minute or two the enemy began to move. Two rockets were fired, one toward us and one toward the river. 'That is their signal for advance, I believe,' General Jackson said. He then ordered all of us down off the parapet but stayed there himself and kept his long glass to his eye sweeping the enemy's line with it from end to end. In a moment he ordered Adair and Carroll to pass word along the line for the men to be ready, to count the enemy's files down as closely as they could, and each to look after his own file-man in their ranks, also, that they should not fire until told and then to aim above the cross-belt plates. . . .

"Then all the guns opened. The British batteries, formed in the left rear of their storming column near the river, were still concealed from us by the fog, but they replied, directing their fire by the sound of our guns. It was a grand sight to see their flashes light up the fog—turning it into the hues of the rainbow.

"Still the enemy came on, but no sound from the rifle-line; no fire but that of artillery on either side. Our Batteries Nos. 7 and 8 were on the rifle-line. Number 7 had an old Spanish 18-pounder and a 6-pounder. Number 8 had but one gun—a 6-pounder. The smoke from these hung in front of the works or drifted slowly toward the enemy without lifting much in the damp air. Adair noticed this and said it was worse than the fog; that the smoke would spoil the aim of the riflemen when their turn came. Carroll agreed with him. Then General Jackson ordered these two batteries to cease firing, whereupon the smoke soon lifted and the head of the enemy's column appeared not more than three hundred to three hundred and fifty yards off and coming on at quick-

---

*From Stanley Clisby Arthur, THE STORY OF THE BATTLE OF NEW ORLEANS, Louisiana Historical Society, 1915.

step, with men in front carrying a few scaling-ladders.

"Suddenly one rifle cracked a little to the left of where I stood. A mounted officer on the right and a little in front of the British head of column reeled in his saddle and fell from his horse headlong to the ground. What followed in an instant I cannot attempt to describe. The British had kept right on, apparently not minding the artillery fire much, though it was rapid and well-directed. They were used to it. But now, when every hunter's rifle from the right of Carroll's line to the edge of the swamp where Coffee stood, was searching for their vitals, the British soldiers stopped! That was something new, something they were not used to!

"They couldn't stand it. In five minutes the whole front of their formation was shaken as if by an earthquake. Not one mounted officer could be seen. Either rider or horse, or both, in every case, was down—most of them dead or dying. I had been in battle where rifles were used up on the northwest frontier under Harrison. But, even so, I had never seen anything like this.

"In less than ten minutes the first line of the enemy's column had disappeared, exposing the second, which was about a hundred yards in its rear. You see, their formation was columns or brigade in battalion front and there were three battalions—or regiments—in the column, each formed four ranks deep. The plain was so level and their formation in line so dense that to a certain extent the front or leading battalion afforded some cover to the one following, and so on.

"When their leading battalion, which we now know to have been the Forty-fourth Regiment, was practically destroyed, the next one, which was the Seventh Regiment, had been already a good deal shaken by the halt and carnage in the first and by the headlong flight of the survivors around or through its ranks, and so the Seventh Regiment broke almost as soon as they got their full weight of our rifle-fire. This left exposed in turn their third regiment of the column which was the Fourth or King's Own Foot, and they, too, succumbed after a very brief experience. Almost, as incredible as it may seem, this whole column, numbering, I should say, 2,500 or 2,600 men, was literally melted down by our rifle-fire. To put it another way, this column had been to all intents destroyed and the work was done in less than twenty minutes from the first rifle-shot. No such execution by small arms was ever done before, and I don't believe it ever will be done again."

Steadily and fast the column of General Gibbs marched toward the batteries numbered six, seven and eight, which played upon it, at first with but occasional effect, often missing, sometimes throwing a ball right into its midst, and causing it to reel and pause for a moment. Promptly were the gaps filled up; bravely the columns came on. As they neared the lines the well-aimed shot made more dreadful havoc, "cutting great lanes in the column from front to rear" and tossing men and parts of men aloft, or hurling them far on one side. At length, still steady and unbroken, they came within range of the small arms, the rifles of Carroll's Tennesseans, the muskets of Adair's Kentuckians—those four lines of sharp-shooters, one behind the other, coolly waiting the word—"fire!"

At first with a certain deliberation, afterwards, in hottest haste, always with deadly effect, the riflemen plied their terrible weapon. The summit of the embankment was a line of spurting fire, except where the great guns showed their liquid, belching flash. The noise was peculiar and altogether indescribable we are told; a rolling, bursting, echoing noise, never to be forgotten by a man who heard it. Along the whole line it blazed and rolled; the British batteries showering rockets over the scene; Patterson's batteries on the other side of the river joining in the hellish concert.

The column of General Gibbs, mowed by the fire of the riflemen, still advanced, Gibbs at its head. As they caught sight of the ditch, some of the officers cried out: "Where is the 44th? If we get to the ditch, we have no means of crossing and scaling the lines!"

"Here comes the 44th! Here comes the 44th!" shouted General Gibbs, adding that if he lived till to-morrow he would hang Mullens on the highest tree in the cypress wood.

Reassured, these heroic men again pressed on, in the face of that murderous, slaughtering fire. But this could not last. With half its number fallen, and all its commanding officers disabled except the general, its pathway strewed with dead and wounded, and the men falling ever faster and faster, the column wavered and reeled (so the American riflemen thought) like a red ship on a tempestuous sea. At about a hundred yards from the lines the front ranks halted, and so threw the column into disorder, Gibbs shouting in the madness of vexation for them to re-form and advance. There was no re-forming under such a fire. Once checked, the column could but break and retreat in confusion. . . .

Just as the troops began to falter, General Pakenham rode up from his post in the rear towards the head of the column.

Meeting parties of the 44th running about distracted, some carrying fascines, others firing, others in headlong flight, their leader nowhere to be seen,

Pakenham strove to restore them to order, and to urge them on the way they were to go.

"For shame," he cried bitterly, "recollect that you are British soldiers. *This* is the road you ought to take!" pointing to the flashing and roaring hell in front.

Riding on, he was soon met by General Gibbs, who said "they will not obey me. They will not follow me."

Taking off his hat, General Pakenham spurred his horse to the front of the wavering columns, amid a torrent of rifle balls, cheering on the troops by voice, by gesture, by example. At that moment, a ball shattered his right arm, and it fell powerless to his side. The next, his horse fell dead upon the field.

* * *

The heroic Pakenham had not far to go to meet his doom. He was three hundred yards from the lines when the real nature of his enterprise seemed to flash upon him; and he turned to Sir John Tylden and said: "Order up the reserve."

Then, seeing the Highlanders advancing to the support of General Gibbs, he, still waving his hat, but waving it now with his left hand, cried out, amidst the deafening din of musketry: "Come on the tartan! Hurrah, brave Highlanders!"

At that moment "I heard a single rifle shot from a group of country carts we had been using," wrote General Jackson, in a personal letter to President Monroe, "and a moment thereafter I saw Pakenham reel and pitch out of his saddle. I have always believed he fell from the bullet of a free man of color, who was a famous rifle shot and came from the Attakapas region of Louisiana. I did not know where General Pakenham was lying or I should have sent to him, or gone in person, to offer any service in my power to render. I was told he lived two hours after he was hit. His wound was directly through the liver and bowels."

* * *

A more painful fate was that of General Gibbs. A few moments after Pakenham fell Gibbs received his death wound, and was carried off the field writhing in agony and uttering fierce imprecations. He lingered all that day and the succeeding night, dying in torment on the morrow in the de la Ronde mansion. Nearly at the same moment General Keane was painfully wounded in the neck and thigh, and was also borne to the rear. Colonel Dale, of the Highlanders,

fulfilled his prophecy and fell at the head of his regiment. The Highlanders, under Major Creagh, wavered not, but advanced steadily, and too slowly, into the very tempest of General Carroll's fire until they were within one hundred yards of the lines. There, for cause unknown, they halted and stood; a huge and glittering target, until five hundred and forty-four of their number had fallen, then they broke and fled in horror and amazement to the rear. The column of General Gibbs did not advance after the fall of their leader. Leaving heaps of slain behind them, they, too, forsook the bloody field, rushed in utter confusion out of the fire, and took refuge at the bottom of the wet ditches and behind trees and bushes on the borders of the swamps.

* * *

"The fire of the Americans from behind their barricade had been indeed most murderous and had caused so sudden a repulse that it was difficult to persuade ourselves that such an event had happened —the whole affair being more like a dream, or some scene of enchantment, than reality."

The scene behind the American works during the fire can be easily imagined. One half of the army never fired a shot. The battalions of Plauche, Daquin and Lacoste, the whole of the forty-fourth regiment, and one-half of the Coffee's Tennesseeans, had nothing to do but to stand still at their posts and chafe with vain impatience for a chance to join in the fight. The Creoles could only with difficulty be restrained from stealing from their post to the right or left to have a shot at the *capotes rouges*. The batteries alone at the center of the works contributed anything to the fortunes of the day. Yet, no; that is not quite correct. The moment the British came into view, and their signal rocket pierced the sky with its fiery train, the band of the Battalion d'Orleans struck up "Yankee Doodle"; and thenceforth, throughout the action, it did not cease to discourse all the national and military airs in which it had been instructed.

At eight-thirty, there being no signs of a renewed attack and no enemy in sight, an order was sent along the lines to cease firing with the small arms. The General, surrounded by his staff, then walked from end to end of the works, stopping at each battery and post, and addressing a few words of congratulation and praise to their defenders. It was a proud, glad moment for these men, when, panting from their two hours' labor, blackened with smoke and sweat, they listened to the General's burning words, and saw the light of victory in his countenance. . . .

Famous Court Decisions
of John Marshall

John Marshall was the fourth Chief Justice of the Supreme Court. He served as Chief Justice from 1801 to 1835. His decisions during that thirty-four year period established principles of interpreting the Constitution which helped to define the relationship between the branches of the federal government and the powers of each.

The following account reviews the impact of Marshall's court decisions and describes the significance of some of his most important decisions. It was written by a United States Commission to celebrate the two-hundredth anniversary of Marshall's birth.*

... Marshall had been in his high post only 2 years when he laid down for the first time in the name of the entire Court the doctrine that the judges have the power to declare an act of Congress null and void when in their opinion it violates the Constitution. This power was not expressly conferred on the Court. Though many able men had held that the judicial branch of the Government enjoyed that power, the principle was not positively and firmly established until 1803, when the case of *Marbury* vs. *Madison*, involving a section of a Federal statute, was decided.

In rendering that historic opinion, Marshall cited no precedents, laid no foundations for his argument in ancient lore. Rather, with that great logic and wisdom which characterized so many of his opinions, did he rest it on the general character of the American system. The Constitution, he wrote, is the supreme law of the land; it controls and binds all who act in the name of the United States; it limits the powers of Congress and defines the rights of citizens. If Congress could ignore its limitations and trespass upon the privileges of citizens, he argued, then the Constitution would disappear and Congress would become sovereign. Since the Constitution must be and is from the nature of things supreme over Congress, it is the duty of judges, under their oath of office, to sustain it against measures which violate it. Therefore, reasoning from the inherent structure of the American constitutional system, the courts must declare null and void all acts which are not authorized. "A law repugnant to the Constitution," he closed, "is void and the courts as well as other depart-

*From the FINAL REPORT OF THE UNITED STATES COMMISSION FOR THE CELEBRATION OF THE TWO-HUNDREDTH ANNIVERSARY OF THE BIRTH OF JOHN MARSHALL, U.S. Government Printing Office, 1956.

ments are bound by that instrument." From that day to this, the practice of Federal and State courts in passing upon the constitutionality of laws has remained unshaken.

Yet at the moment this doctrine was received by Jefferson and many of his followers with consternation. If the idea that the Court could declare Federal laws null and void was sound, he exclaimed: "then indeed is our Constitution a complete suicide. For, intending to establish three departments, coordinate and independent, that they might check and balance one another, it has given, according to this opinion, to one of them alone the right to prescribe rules for the government of the others, and to that one, too, which is unelected by and independent of the nation. . . . The Constitution, on this hypothesis, is a mere thing of wax in the hands of the judiciary, which they may twist and shape into any form they please." But Marshall was persuasive and his view prevailed, though from time to time, other men, clinging to Jefferson's opinion, likewise opposed judicial exercise of the high power proclaimed in *Marbury* vs. *Madison*.

Had Marshall stopped with declaring unconstitutional an act of Congress, he would have heard less criticism from political opponents; but, with the same firmness, he set aside important acts of State legislatures as well, whenever, in his opinion, they violated the Federal Constitution. In 1810, in the case of *Fletcher* vs. *Peck*, he annulled a law of the Georgia Legislature, informing the State that it was not sovereign, but a "part of a large empire . . . a member of the American Union; and that Union has a Constitution . . . which imposes limits to the legislatures of the several States."

In the case of *McCulloch* vs. *Maryland*, decided in 1819, the Chief Justice declared void an act of the Maryland Legislature designed to paralyze the branches of the United States Bank established in that State. He reiterated then his oft-repeated theme: "The government of the U.S. then, though limited in its powers, is supreme; and its laws, when made in pursuance of the Constitution, form the supreme law of the land, anything in the constitution or laws of any State to the contrary notwithstanding."

Also in 1819, in the still more memorable *Dartmouth College* case, he abrogated an act of the New Hampshire Legislature which infringed upon a charter received by the college from King George long before. That charter, he asserted, was a contract between the State and the college, the obligation of which under the Federal Constitution no legislature could impair. Without the decision in the *Dartmouth* case, it is probable that our whole system of higher education would have developed in quite a different way than it has. If Dartmouth could have been summarily taken over by a State, then so could Harvard or Columbia, Princeton or Yale, Duke or Stanford.

Two years later, Marshall stirred the wrath of Virginia by summoning her to the bar of the Supreme Court to answer in a case involving the validity of one of her laws; and then he justified his action in a powerful opinion rendered in the case of *Cohens* vs *Virginia*. "A constitution is framed for ages to come and is designed to approach immortality as nearly as human institutions can approach it," the Chief Justice wrote. "Its course cannot always be tranquil. It is exposed to storms and tempests, and its framers must be unwise statesmen indeed if they have not provided it, so far as its nature will permit, with the means of self-preservation from the perils it may be destined to encounter. No government ought to be so defective in its organization as not to contain within itself the means of securing of its own laws against other dangers than those which occur every day. . . .

> In war we are one people. In making peace we are one people. In all commercial regulations we are one and the same people. In many other respects the American people are one, and the government which is alone capable of controlling and managing their interests in all these respects is the government of the Union. It is their government, and in that character they have no other.
>
> America has chosen to be, in many respects and to many purposes, a nation; and for all these purposes her government is complete; to all these objects it is competent. The people have declared that in the exercise of all the powers given for these objects it is supreme. It can, then, in effecting these objects, legitimately control all individuals or governments within the American territory. The constitution and laws of a State, so far as they are repugnant to the Constitution and laws of the United States, are absolutely void. These States are constituent parts of the United States. They are members of one great empire—for some purposes sovereign, for some purposes subordinate.

All these opinions aroused the legislatures of the States, especially those in control of non-Federalists. They passed sheaves of resolutions protesting and condemning; but Marshall never turned and never backed down. The Constitution of the United States, he fairly thundered at them, is the supreme law of the land; the Supreme Court is the proper tribunal to pass finally upon the validity of the laws of the States; and "those sovereignties," far from possessing the right of review and nullification, are irrevocably bound by the decisions of the Court. This was strong medicine for the authors of the Kentucky and Virginia Resolutions and for the members of the Hartford convention; but they had to swallow it.

While restricting Congress in the *Marbury* case and the State legislatures in a score of cases, Marshall also laid the judicial foundation for a broad and liberal view of the Constitution as opposed to narrow and strict construction. As he said in his opinion in the *Gibbons* vs. *Ogden* case (1824): "This instrument contains an enumeration of powers expressly granted by the people to their government. It has been said that these powers ought to be construed strictly. But why ought they to be so construed? Is there one sentence in the Constitution which gives countenance to this rule?"

In *McCulloch* vs. *Maryland*, he construed the words "necessary and proper" in such a way as to confer upon Congress a wide range of "implied powers" in addition to its express powers. Since the case involved, among other things, the question whether the act establishing the second United States Bank was authorized by the Constitution, Marshall felt impelled to settle the issue by a sweeping and affirmative opinion. Congress, he argued, has large powers over taxation and the currency; a bank is of appropriate use in the exercise of its enumerated powers; and therefore, though not absolutely necessary, a bank is entirely proper and constitutional.

"With respect to the means by which the powers that the Constitution confers are to be carried into execution," Marshall said, Congress must be allowed the discretion which "will enable that body to perform the high duties assigned to it, in the manner most beneficial to the people." In short, the Constitution of the United States is not a straitjacket but a flexible instrument vesting in the national legislature full authority to meet national problems as they arise. In delivering this opinion, Marshall used language almost identical with that employed by Lincoln years later when, standing on the battlefield of Gettysburg, he declared that "government of the people, by the people, for the people, shall not perish from the earth."

Marshall in his arguments drew much from his colleagues, especially his devoted adherent, Justice Story; and he was stimulated and inspired by the lawyers pleading before the Court, among them some of the most brilliant legal minds America has seen, including Daniel Webster, Luther Martin, William Pinkney, William Wirt, and Jeremiah Mason. So great was his winning charm and his absolute integrity that he gained the admiration of his enemies and the undoubted affection of his friends. He had a fine literary style, combining concise clarity with glowing simplicity.

The Chief Justice had strong feelings about the importance of an independent judiciary at both Federal and State levels. In 1829 he had occasion to speak on the subject as follows:

> Advert, sir, to the duties of a judge—he has to pass between the Government and the man whom that Government is prosecuting; between the most powerful individual in the community, and the poorest and most unpopular. . . . The Judicial Department comes home in its effects to every man's fireside; it passes on his property, his reputation, his life, his all. Is it not, to the last degree important, that he should be rendered perfectly and completely independent, with nothing to influence or control him but God and his conscience? You do not allow a man to perform the duties of a juryman or a judge, if he has one dollar of interest in the matter to be decided; and will you allow a Judge to give a decision when his office may depend upon it? when his decision may offend a powerful and influential man? . . . If they may be removed at pleasure, will any lawyer of distinction come upon your bench? No, sir. I have always thought, from my earliest youth till now, that the greatest scourge an angry heaven could ever inflict upon an ungrateful and sinning people, was an ignorant, a corrupt, or a dependent Judiciary.

The influence of John Marshall extended not only across the Nation, but over the whole world; and in this day when foreign affairs and international law are of ever greater importance, it is appropriate to close this brief essay with the words of the late John Bassett Moore, first American jurist to sit as a judge of the Permanent Court of International Justice, who said of Marshall:

He is known in other lands as the author of important opinions on questions which deeply concern the welfare and intercourse of all nations. In the treatment of questions of international law he exhibited the same traits of mind, the same breadth and originality of thought, the same power in discovering and the same certainty in applying fundamental principles, that distinguished him in the realm of constitutional discussions; and it was his lot in more than one case to blaze the way in the establishment of rules of international conduct.

Monroe's Messages on Florida

After the purchase of the Louisiana Territory in 1803, many Americans desired further expansion into Florida, which was held by Spain. The expansionist feeling was increased after the War of 1812 when it was found that the Spanish could no longer control the area.

The following messages to Congress, given by President Monroe from 1818 to 1820, describe American problems with the Spanish concerning Florida, General Andrew Jackson's march into the peninsula, and the terms of a United States—Spanish agreement ceding the Floridas to the United States.*

Our relations with Spain remain nearly in the state in which they were at the close of the last session. The convention of 1802, providing for the adjustment of a certain portion of the claims of our citizens for injuries sustained by spoliation, and so long suspended by the Spanish Government, has at length been ratified by it, but no arrangement has yet been made for the payment of another portion of like claims, not less extensive or well founded, or for other classes of claims, or for the settlement of boundaries. These subjects have again been brought under consideration in both countries, but no agreement has been entered into respecting them. In the meantime events have occurred which clearly prove the ill effect of the policy which that Government has so long pursued on the friendly relations of the two countries, which it is presumed is at least of as much importance to Spain as to the United States to maintain. A state of things has existed in the Floridas the tendency of which has been obvious to all who have paid the slightest attention to the progress of affairs in that quarter. Throughout the whole of those Provinces to which the Spanish title extends the Government of Spain has scarcely been felt. Its authority has been confined almost exclusively to the walls of Pensacola and St. Augustine, within which only small garrisons have been maintained. Adventurers from every country, fugitives from justice, and absconding slaves have found an asylum there. Several tribes of Indians, strong in the number of their warriors, remarkable for their ferocity, and whose settlements extend to our limits, inhabit those Provinces. These different hordes of people, connected together, disregarding on the one side the authority of Spain, and protected on the other by an imaginary line which separates Florida from the United States, have violated our laws prohibiting the introduction of

*From Monroe's Second Annual Message to Congress and Special Message of May 9, 1820, Old South Leaflet No. 129, Vol. VI. Reprinted by courtesy of the Old South Association in Boston.

slaves, have practiced various frauds on our revenue, and committed every kind of outrage on our peaceable citizens which their proximity to us enabled them to perpetrate. The invasion of Amelia Island last year by a small band of adventurers, not exceeding 150 in number, who wrested it from the inconsiderable Spanish force stationed there, and held it several months, during which a single feeble effort only was made to recover it, which failed, clearly proves how completely extinct the Spanish authority had become, as the conduct of those adventurers while in possession of the island as distinctly shows the pernicious purposes for which their combination had been formed.

This country had, in fact, become the theater of every species of lawless adventure. With little population of its own, the Spanish authority almost extinct, and the colonial governments in a state of revolution, having no pretension to it, and sufficiently employed in their own concerns, it was in a great measure derelict, and the object of cupidity to every adventurer. A system of buccaneering was rapidly organizing over it which menaced in its consequences the lawful commerce of every nation, and particularly of the United States, while it presented a temptation to every people, on whose seduction its success principally depended. In regard to the United States, the pernicious effect of this unlawful combination was not confined to the ocean; the Indian tribes have constituted the effective force in Florida. With these tribes these adventurers had formed at an early period a connection with a view to avail themselves of that force to promote their own projects of accumulation and aggrandizement. It is to the interference of some of these adventurers, in misrepresenting the claims and titles of the Indians to land and in practising on their savage propensities, that the Seminole war is principally to be traced. Men who thus connect themselves with savage communities and stimulate them to war, which is always attended on their part with acts of barbarity the most shocking, deserve to be viewed in a worse light than the savages. They would certainly have no claim to an immunity from the punishment which, according to the rules of warfare practiced by the savages, might justly be inflicted on the savages themselves. . . .

In authorizing Major General Jackson to enter Florida in pursuit of the Seminoles care was taken not to encroach on the rights of Spain. I regret to have to add that in executing this order facts were disclosed respecting the conduct of the officers of Spain in authority there in encouraging the war, furnishing munitions of war and other supplies to carry it on, and in other acts not less marked which

evinced their participation in the hostile purposes of that combination and justified the confidence with which it inspired the savages that by those officers they would be protected. A conduct so incompatible with the friendly relations existing between the two countries, particularly with the positive obligation of the fifth article of the treaty of 1795, by which Spain was bound to restrain, even by force, those savages from acts of hostility against the United States, could not fail to excite surprise.

* * *

Instigated by the English emissaries Nichols and Woodbine, the Seminoles, with scattering bands from other tribes, continued to annoy the border settlements in Georgia, and several times attacked transports on the Apalachicola River, in one instance mustering twelve hundred men and continuing the fight for several days. In January, 1818, General Jackson made a treaty with the Creeks, and engaged them to join him in attack upon the Seminoles of Florida. In the spring of the same year, with a force of one thousand militia, five hundred regulars, and nearly two thousand Indians, he started on an expedition against the Seminoles, with the purpose of destroying their power and putting an end to their depredations.

Marching rapidly upon the Miccosukee towns of East Florida, he destroyed them, and soon afterwards attacked and destroyed the Fowl towns, the Indians making but a feeble resistance. General Jackson then marched upon St. Mark's, which was strongly fortified and had twenty guns mounted. The fort surrendered without resistance, and Prophet Francis and another Indian chief fell into the hands of the Americans, and were immediately hanged.

At Miccosukee, General Jackson found three hundred scalps of men, women, and children, most of them fresh, and which had evidently been recently exhibited with triumph. From St. Mark's, General Jackson marched to Suwanee, where he dispersed a large number of Indians, and took many prisoners, among them two Englishmen, Arbuthnot and Ambrister, who were accused of being the chief agents in supplying the Indians with arms and ammunition and directing their operations against the whites. A court-martial was held to try them, and both being found guilty were sentenced to suffer death, one by hanging, the other to be shot, and the sentence was promptly executed. This action of General Jackson was severely criticised, both at the time, and subsequently in the political contests in which he became engaged. General Jackson afterwards marched against Pensacola, having been informed that the Spanish government, while furnishing arms to the Indians who were hostile to the United States, refused to allow provisions to pass up the Escambia for the American troops. Upon the approach of General Jackson, the Spanish governor retired to Fort Barrancas, which, being menaced by the United States troops, was surrendered after a slight show of resistance.

A treaty of peace, consisting of sixteen articles, was concluded between Spain and the United States on the 22d of February, 1819, ceding the Floridas to the United States. The sixth article of this treaty provided that "the inhabitants of the territories ceded to the United States should be incorporated into the Union of the United States, as soon as might be consistent with the principles of the Federal Constitution, and admitted to the enjoyment of all the privileges, rights, and immunities of the citizens of the United States."

The eighth article provided "that all the grants of land made before the 24th of January, 1818, by Spain, should be ratified and confirmed to the same extent that the same grants would be valid if the territories had remained under the dominion of Spain."

The ninth article provided that "the United States would cause satisfaction to be made for the injuries, if any, which by process of law should be established to have been suffered by the Spanish officers and individual Spanish inhabitants by the late operations of the American army in Florida."

These articles of the treaty have given validity to what are now known as Spanish grants and claims for losses, in which so many of the people of Florida were interested.

The treaty was finally ratified on the 19th of February, 1821. The change of flags in East Florida took place at St. Augustine, 10th of July, 1821, under Governor Coppinger on the part of Spain, and Colonel Robert Butler on the part of the United States; in West Florida, at Pensacola, on the 21st of July, 1821, Governor Callava representing the Spanish government, and General Jackson that of the United States.

The Monroe Doctrine

The Monroe Doctrine as announced on December 2, 1823 has held a special place in American foreign policy. The Monroe Doctrine was simply a policy of a particular president. It was not a treaty; it was never debated in Congress; it was never considered a part of international law.

The following extracts from Monroe's inaugural addresses and annual messages trace the development of the doctrine between 1817 and 1824.

President Monroe wanted to keep the Western Hemisphere free from European interference and the United States free from entanglements with the nations of Europe.*

[March 4, 1817.] Dangers from abroad are not less deserving of attention. Experiencing the fortune of other nations, the United States may be again involved in war, and it may in that event be the object of the adverse party to overset our Government, to break our Union, and demolish us as a nation. Our distance from Europe and the just, moderate, and pacific policy of our Government may form some security against these dangers, but they ought to be anticipated and guarded against....

[December 2, 1817.] It was anticipated at an early stage that the contest between Spain and the colonies would become highly interesting to the United States. It was natural that our citizens should sympathize in events which affected their neighbors. It seemed probable also that the prosecution of the conflict along our coast and in contiguous countries would occasionally interrupt our commerce and otherwise affect the persons and property of our citizens. These anticipations have been realized. Such injuries have been received from persons acting under authority of both the parties, and for which redress has in most instances been withheld. Through every stage of the conflict the United States have maintained an impartial neutrality, giving aid to neither of the parties in men, money, ships, or munitions of war. They have regarded the contest not in the light of an ordinary insurrection or rebellion, but as a civil war between parties nearly equal, having as to neutral powers equal rights. Our ports have been open to both, and every article the fruit of our soil or of the industry of our citizens which either was permitted to take has been equally free to the other. Should the colonies establish their independence, it is proper now to state that this Government neither seeks nor would accept from them any advantage in commerce or otherwise which will not be equally open to all other nations. The colonies will in that event become independent states, free from any obligation to or connection with us which it may not then be their interest to form on the basis of a fair reciprocity....

---

*The Development of the Monroe Doctrine as Monroe Stated It in Albert Bushnell Hart (ed.), AMERICAN HISTORY TOLD BY CONTEMPORARIES, Vol. III, Macmillan Company, 1901.

[November 16, 1818.] By a circular note addressed by the ministers of Spain to the allied powers, with whom they are respectively accredited, it appears that the allies have undertaken to mediate between Spain and the South American Provinces, and that the manner and extent of their interposition would be settled by a congress which was to have met at Aix-la-Chapelle in September last. From the general policy and course of proceeding observed by the allied powers in regard to this contest it is inferred that they will confine their interposition to the expression of their sentiments, abstaining from the application of force. I state this impression that force will not be applied with the greater satisfaction because it is a course more consistent with justice and likewise authorizes a hope that the calamities of the war will be confined to the parties only, and will be of shorter duration.

From the view taken of this subject, founded on all the information that we have been able to obtain, there is good cause to be satisfied with the course heretofore pursued by the United States in regard to this contest, and to conclude that it is proper to adhere to it, especially in the present state of affairs. . . .

[December 7, 1819.] This contest has from its commencement been very interesting to other powers, and to none more so than to the United States. A virtuous people may and will confine themselves within the limit of a strict neutrality; but it is not in their power to behold a conflict so vitally important to their neighbors without the sensibility and sympathy which naturally belong to such a case. It has been the steady purpose of this Government to prevent that feeling leading to excess, and it is very gratifying to have it in my power to state that so strong has been the sense throughout the whole community of what was due to the character and obligations of the nation that very few examples of a contrary kind have occurred.

The distance of the colonies from the parent country and the great extent of their population and resources gave them advantages which it was anticipated at a very early period would be difficult for Spain to surmount. The steadiness, consistency, and success with which they have pursued their object, as evinced more particularly by the undisturbed sovereignty which Buenos Ayres has so long enjoyed, evidently gave them a strong claim to the favorable consideration of other nations. These sentiments on the part of the United States have not been withheld from other powers, with whom it is desirable to act in concert. Should it become manifest to the world that the efforts of Spain to subdue these Provinces will be fruitless, it may be presumed that the Spanish Government itself will give up the contest. In producing such a determination it can not be doubted that the opinion of friendly powers who have taken no part in the controversy will have their merited influence. . . .

[November 14, 1820.) . . . No facts are known to this Government to warrant the belief that any of the powers of Europe will take part in the contest, whence it may be inferred, considering all circumstances which must have weight in producing the result, that an adjustment will finally take place on the basis proposed by the colonies. To promote that result by friendly counsels with other powers, including Spain herself, has been the uniform policy of this Government. . . .

[March 5, 1821.] This contest was considered at an early stage by my predecessor a civil war in which the parties were entitled to equal rights in our ports. This decision, the first made by any power, being formed on great consideration of the comparative strength and resources of the parties, the length of time, and successful opposition made by the colonies, and of all other circumstances on which it ought to depend, was in strict accord with the law of nations. . . .

[December 3, 1821.] . . . It has long been manifest that it would be impossible for Spain to reduce these colonies by force, and equally so that no conditions short of their independence would be satisfactory to them. It may therefore be presumed, and it is earnestly hoped, that the Government of Spain, guided by enlightened and liberal councils, will find it to comport with its interests and due to its magnanimity to terminate this exhausting controversy on that basis. To promote this result by friendly counsel with the Government of Spain will be the object of the Government of the United States. . . .

[December 2, 1823.] At the proposal of the Russian Imperial Government, made through the minister of the Emperor residing here, a full power and instructions have been transmitted to the minister of the United States at St. Petersburg to arrange by amicable negotiation the respective rights and interests of the two nations on the northwest coast of this continent. . . . In the discussions to which this interest has given rise and in the arrangements by which they may terminate the occasion has been judged proper for asserting, as a principle in which the rights and interests of the United States are involved, that the American continents, by the free and independent condition which they have assumed and maintain, are henceforth not to be considered as subjects for future colonization by any European powers. . . .

. . . The citizens of the United States cherish sentiments the most friendly in favor of the liberty and happiness of their fellow-men on that side of the Atlantic. In the wars of the European powers in matters relating to themselves we have never taken any part, nor does it comport with our policy so to do. It is only when our rights are invaded or seriously menaced that we resent injuries or make preparation for our defense. With the movements in this hemisphere we are of necessity more immediately connected, and by causes which must be obvious to all enlightened and impartial observers. The political system of the allied powers is essentially different in this respect from that of America. This difference proceeds from that which exists in their respective Governments; and to the defense of our own, which has been achieved by the loss of so much blood and treasure, and matured by the wisdom of their most enlightened citizens, and under which we have enjoyed unexampled felicity, this whole nation is devoted. We owe it, therefore, to candor and to the amicable relations existing between the United States and those powers to declare that we should consider any attempt on their part to extend their system to any portion of this hemisphere as dangerous to our peace and safety. With the existing colonies or dependencies of any European power we have not interfered and shall not interfere. But with the Governments who have declared their independence and maintained it, and whose independence we have, on great consideration and on just principles, acknowledged, we could not view any interposition for the purpose of oppressing them, or controlling in any other manner their destiny, by any European power in any other light than as the manifestation of an unfriendly disposition toward the United States. . . .

. . . Our policy in regard to Europe, which was adopted at an early stage of the wars which have so long agitated that quarter of the globe, nevertheless remains the same, which is, not to interfere in the internal concerns of any of its powers; to consider the government *de facto* as the legitimate government for us; to cultivate friendly relations with it, and to preserve those relations by a frank, firm, and manly policy, meeting in all instances the just claims of every power, submitting to injuries from none. But in regard to those continents circumstances are eminently and conspicuously different. It is impossible that the allied powers should extend their political system to any portion of either continent without endangering our peace and happiness; nor can anyone believe that our southern brethren, if left to themselves, would adopt it of their own accord. It is equally impossible, therefore, that we should behold such interposition in any form with indifference. . . .

[December 7, 1824.] . . . these new States are settling down under Governments elective and representative in every branch, similar to our own. In this course we ardently wish them to persevere, under a firm conviction that it will promote their happiness. In this, their career, however, we have not interfered, believing that every people have a right to institute for themselves the government which in their judgment, may suit them best. Our example is before them, of the good effect of which, being our neighbors, they are competent judges, and to their judgment we leave it, in the expectation that other powers will pursue the same policy. The deep interest which we take in their independence, which we have acknowledged, and in their enjoyment of all the rights incident thereto, especially in the very important one of instituting their own Governments, has been declared, and is known to the world. Separated as we are from Europe by the great Atlantic Ocean, we can have no concern in the wars of the European Governments nor in the causes which produce them. The balance of power between them, into whichever scale it may turn in its various vibrations, can not affect us. It is the interest of the United States to preserve the most friendly relations with every power and on conditions fair, equal, and applicable to all. But in regard to our neighbors our situation is different. It is impossible for the European Governments to interfere in their concerns, especially in those alluded to, which are vital, without affecting us; indeed, the motive which might induce such interference in the present state of the war between the parties, if a war it may be called, would appear to be equally applicable to us. It is gratifying to know that some of the powers with whom we enjoy a very friendly intercourse, and to whom these views have been communicated, have appeared to acquiesce in them.

The Majority Is to Govern

Andrew Jackson was elected president in 1828 and in December 1829, he delivered his first annual message to Congress. In that message, Jackson set forth his faith in democracy.*

I consider it one of the most urgent of my duties to bring to your attention the propriety of amending that part of our Constitution which relates to the election of President and Vice President. Our system of government was, by its framers, deemed an experiment; and they, therefore, consistently provided a mode of remedying its defects.

To the People belongs the right of electing their

---

*SENATE DOCUMENTS (1829-1830), I, Document 1.

Chief Magistrate: it was never designed that their choice should, in any case, be defeated, either by the intervention of electoral colleges, or by the agency confided, under certain contingencies, to the House of Representatives. Experience proves, that, in proportion as agents to execute the will of the People are multiplied, there is danger of their wishes being frustrated. Some may be unfaithful: all are liable to err. So far, therefore, as the People can, with convenience, speak, it is safer for them to express their own will.

The number of aspirants to the Presidency, and the diversity of the interests which may influence their claims, leave little reason to expect a choice in the first instance: and, in that event, the election must devolve on the House of Representatives, where, it is obvious, the will of the People may not be always ascertained; or, if ascertained, may not be regarded. From the mode of voting by States, the choice is to be made by twenty-four votes; and it may often occur, that one of these will be controlled by an individual representative. Honors and offices are at the disposal of the successful candidate. Repeated ballotings may make it apparent that a single individual holds the cast in his hand. May he not be tempted to name his reward? But even without corruption—supposing the probity of the Representative to be proof against the powerful motives by which it may be assailed—the will of the People is still constantly liable to be misrepresented. One may err from ignorance of the wishes of his constituents; another, from a conviction that it is his duty to be governed by his own judgment of the fitness of the candidates: finally, although all were inflexibly honest—all accurately informed of the wishes of their constituents—yet, under the present mode of election, a minority may often elect the President; and when this happens, it may reasonably be expected that efforts will be made on the part of the majority to rectify this injurious operation of their institutions. But although no evil of this character should result from such a perversion of the first principle of our system—*that the majority is to govern*—it must be very certain that a President elected by a minority cannot enjoy the confidence necessary to the successful discharge of his duties.

In this, as in all other matters of public concern, policy requires that as few impediments as possible should exist to the free operation of the public will. Let us, then, endeavor so to amend our system, that the office of Chief Magistrate may not be conferred upon any citizen but in pursuance of a fair expression of the will of the majority.

I would therefore recommend such an amendment of the Constitution as may remove all intermediate agency in the election of President and Vice President. The mode may be so regulated as to preserve to each State its present relative weight in the election; and a failure in the first attempt may be provided for, by confining the second to a choice between the two highest candidates. In connexion with such an amendment, it would seem advisable to limit the service of the Chief Magistrate to a single term, of either four or six years. If, however, it should not be adopted, it is worthy of consideration whether a provision disqualifying for office the Representatives in Congress on whom such an election may have devolved, would not be proper.

While members of Congress can be constitutionally appointed to offices of trust and profit, it will be the practice, even under the most conscientious adherence to duty, to select them for such stations as they are believed to be better qualified to fill than other citizens; but the purity of our Government would doubtless be promoted, by their exclusion from all appointments in the gift of the President in whose election they may have been officially concerned. The nature of the judicial office, and the necessity of securing in the Cabinet and in diplomatic stations of the highest rank, the best talents and political experience, should, perhaps, except these from the exclusion.

There are perhaps few men who can for any great length of time enjoy office and power, without being more or less under the influence of feelings unfavorable to the faithful discharge of their public duties. Their integrity may be proof against improper considerations immediately addressed to themselves; but they are apt to acquire a habit of looking with indifference upon the public interests, and of tolerating conduct from which an unpractised man would revolt. Office is considered as a species of property; and Government, rather as a means of promoting individual interests, than as an instrument created solely for the service of the People. Corruption in some, and, in others, a perversion of correct feelings and principles, divert Government from its legitimate ends, and make it an engine for the support of the few at the expense of the many. The duties of all public officers are, or, at least, admit of being made, so plain and simple, that men of intelligence may readily qualify themselves for their performance; and I cannot but believe that more is lost by the long continuance of men in office, than is generally to be gained by their experience. I submit therefore to your consideration, whether the efficiency of the Government would not be promoted, and official industry and integrity better secured, by a general extension of the law which limits appointments to four years.

In a country where offices are created solely for the benefit of the People, no one man has any more intrinsic right to official station than another. Offices were not established to give support to particular men, at the public expense. No individual wrong is therefore done by removal, since neither appointment to, nor continuance in, office, is a matter of right. The incumbent became an officer with a view to public benefits; and when these require his removal, they are not to be sacrificed to private interests. It is the People, and they alone, who have a right to complain, when a bad officer is substituted for a good one. He who is removed has the same means of obtaining a living, that are enjoyed by the millions who never held office. The proposed limitation would destroy the idea of property, now so generally connected with official station; and although individual distress may be sometimes produced, it would, by promoting that rotation which constitutes a leading principle in the republican creed, give healthful action to the system.

* * *

Democracy in America

Alexis de Tocqueville (1805-1859) was a French aristocrat who came to America in 1830 to study liberty and democracy in the young nation. Deeply impressed with what he saw, de Tocqueville returned to France and published *Democracy in America* in 1835. The book was an outstanding description of the American way of life and it helped to spread democratic ideals throughout Europe.*

Among the novel objects that attracted my attention during my stay in the United States, nothing struck me more forcibly than the general equality of conditions. I readily discovered the prodigious influence which this primary fact exercises on the whole course of society, by giving a certain direction to public opinion, and a certain tenor to the laws; by imparting new maxims to the governing powers, and peculiar habits to the governed.

I speedily perceived that the influence of this fact extends far beyond the political character and the laws of the country, and that it has no less empire over civil society than over the government; it creates opinions, engenders sentiments, suggests the ordinary practices of life, and modifies whatever it does not produce.

*Alexis de Tocqueville, THE REPUBLIC OF THE UNITED STATES OF AMERICA AND ITS POLITICAL INSTITUTIONS, REVIEWED AND EXAMINED, translated by Henry Reeves, New York, 1856, Vols. I & II.

The more I advanced in the study of American society, the more I perceived that the equality of conditions is the fundamental fact from which all others seem to be derived, and the central point at which all my observations constantly terminated.

I then turned my thoughts to our own hemisphere, where I imagined that I discerned something analogous to the spectacle which the New World presented to me. I observed that the equality of conditions is daily advancing toward those extreme limits which it seems to have reached in the United States; and that the democracy which governs the American communities, appears to be rapidly rising into power in Europe.

* * *

THE PRINCIPLE OF THE SOVEREIGNTY OF THE PEOPLE IN AMERICA

Whenever the political laws of the United States are to be discussed, it is with the doctrine of the sovereignty of the people that we must begin.

The principle of the sovereignty of the people, which is to be found, more or less, at the bottom of almost all human institutions, generally remains concealed from view. It is obeyed without being recognised, or if for a moment it be brought to light, it is hastily cast back into the gloom of the sanctuary.

"The will of the nation" is one of those expressions which have been most profusely abused by the wily and the despotic of every age. To the eyes of some it has been represented by the venal suffrages of a few of the satellites of power; to others, by the votes of a timid or an interested minority; and some have even discovered it in the silence of a people, on the supposition that the fact of submission established the right of command.

In America, the principle of the sovereignty of the people is not either barren or concealed, as it is with some other nations; it is recognised by the customs and proclaimed by the laws; it spreads freely, and arrives without impediment at its most remote consequences. . . .

At the present day the principle of the sovereignty of the people has acquired, in the United States, all the practical development which the imagination can conceive. It is unencumbered by those fictions which have been thrown over it in other countries, and it appears in every possible form according to the exigency of the occasion. Sometimes the laws are made by the people in a body, as at Athens; and sometimes its representatives, chosen by universal suffrage, transact business in its name, and almost under its immediate control.

* * *

WHY THE PEOPLE MAY STRICTLY BE SAID TO GOVERN IN THE UNITED STATES

In America the people appoints the legislative and the executive power, and furnishes the jurors who punish all offences against the laws. The American institutions are democratic, not only in their principle but in all their consequences; and the people elects its representatives *directly*, and for the most part *annually*, in order to ensure their dependance. The people is therefore the real directing power; and although the form of government is representative, it is evident that the opinions, the prejudices, the interests, and even the passions of the community are hindered by no durable obstacles from exercising a perpetual influence on society. In the United States the majority governs in the name of the people, as is the case in all the countries in which the people is supreme. This majority is principally composed of peaceable citizens, who, either by inclination or by interest, are sincerely desirous of the welfare of their country.

* * *

OF THE PRINCIPAL SOURCE OF BELIEF AMONG DEMOCRATIC NATIONS

...In the United States the majority undertakes to supply a multitude of ready-made opinions for the use of individuals, who are thus relieved from the necessity of forming opinions of their own. Everybody there adopts great numbers of theories on philosophy, morals, and politics, without inquiry, upon public trust; and if we look to it very narrowly, it will be perceived that religion herself holds her sway there, much less as a doctrine of revelation than as a commonly received opinion.

The fact that the political laws of the Americans are such that the majority rules the community with sovereign sway, materially increases the power which that majority naturally exercises over the mind. For nothing is more customary in man than to recognise superior wisdom in the person of his oppressor. This political omnipotence of the majority in the United States doubtless augments the influence which public opinion would obtain without it over the mind of each member of the community; but the foundations of that influence do not rest upon it. They must be sought for in the principle of equality itself, not in the more or less popular institutions which men living under that condition may give themselves. The intellectual dominion of the greater number would probably be less absolute among a democratic people governed by a king than in the sphere of a pure democracy, but it will always be extremely absolute; and by whatever political laws men are governed in the ages of equality, it may be foreseen that faith in public opinion will become a species of religion there, and the majority its ministering prophet.

Thus intellectual authority will be different, but it will not be diminished; and far from thinking that it will disappear, I augur that it may readily acquire too much preponderance, and confine the action of private judgement within narrower limits than are suited either to the greatness or the happiness of the human race. In the principle of equality I very clearly discern two tendencies; the one leading the mind of every man to untried thoughts, the other inclined to prohibit him from thinking at all. And I perceive how, under the dominion of certain laws, democracy would extinguish that liberty of the mind to which a democratic social condition is favorable; so that, after having broken all the bondage once imposed on it by ranks or by men, the human mind would be closely fettered to the general will of the greatest number.

If the absolute power of a majority were to be substituted by democratic nations, for all the different powers which checked or retarded overmuch the energy of individual minds, the evil would only have changed its symptoms. Men would not have found the means of independent life; they would simply have invented (no easy task) a new dress for servitude. There is—and I cannot repeat it too often—there is in this matter for profound reflection for those who look on freedom as a holy thing, and who hate not only the despot, but despotism.

* * *

WHY DEMOCRATIC NATIONS SHOW A MORE ARDENT AND ENDURING LOVE OF EQUALITY THAN OF LIBERTY

The first and most intense passion which is engendered by the equality of conditions is, I need hardly say, the love of that same equality. My readers will therefore not be surprised that I speak of it before all others.

Everybody has remarked, that in our time, and especially in France, this passion for equality is every day gaining ground in the human heart. It has been said a hundred times that our contemporaries are far more ardently and tenaciously attached to equality than to freedom; but, as I do not find that the causes of the fact have been sufficiently analyzed, I shall endeavour to point them out.

It is possible to imagine an extreme point at which freedom and equality would meet and be confounded together. Let us suppose that all the members of the community take a part in the government, and that each one of them has an equal right to take a part in it. As none is different from his fellows, none can exercise a tyrannical power: men will be perfectly free, because they will all be entirely equal; and they will all be perfectly equal, because they will be entirely free. To this ideal state democratic nations tend. Such is the completest form that equality can assume upon earth; but there are a thousand others which, without being equally perfect, are not less cherished by those nations.

The principle of equality may be established in civil society, without prevailing in the political world. Equal rights may exist of indulging in the same pleasures, of entering the same professions, of frequenting the same places—in a word, of living in the same manner and seeking wealth by the same means, although all men do not take an equal share in the government.

A kind of equality may even be established in the political world, though there should be no political freedom there. A man may be the equal of all his countrymen save one, who is the master of all without distinction, and who selects equally from among them all the agents of his power.

Several other combinations might be easily imagined, by which very great equality would be united to institutions more or less free, or even to institutions wholly without freedom.

Although men cannot become absolutely equal unless they be entirely free, and consequently equality, pushed to its furthest extent, may be confounded with freedom, yet there is good reason for distinguishing the one from the other. The taste which men have for liberty, and that which they feel for equality, are, in fact, two different things; and I am not afraid to add, that, among democratic nations, they are two unequal things.

Upon close inspection, it will be seen that there is in every age some peculiar and preponderating fact with which all others are connected; this fact almost always gives birth to some pregnant idea or some ruling passion, which attracts to itself, and bears away in its course, all the feelings and opinions of the time: it is like a great stream, toward which each of the surrounding rivulets seem to flow.

Freedom has appeared in the world at different times and under various forms; it has not been exclusively bound to any social condition, and it is not confined to democracies. Freedom cannot, therefore, form the distinguishing characteristic of democratic ages. The peculiar and preponderating fact which marks those ages as its own is the equality of conditions; the ruling passion of men in those periods is the love of this equality. Ask not what singular charm the men of democratic ages find in being equal, or what special reasons they may have for clinging so tenaciously to equality rather than to the other advantages which society holds out to them; equality is the distinguishing characteristic of the age they live in; that, of itself, is enough to explain that they prefer it to all the rest.

But independently of this reason there are several others, which will at all times habitually lead men to prefer equality to freedom.

If a people could ever succeed in destroying, or even in diminishing, the equality which prevails in its own body, this could only be accomplished by long and laborious efforts. Its social condition must be modified, its laws abolished, its opinions superseded, its habits changed, its manners corrupted. But political liberty is more easily lost; to neglect to hold it fast, is to allow it to escape.

Men therefore not only cling to equality because it is dear to them; they also adhere to it because they think it will last for ever.

That political freedom may compromise in its excesses the tranquillity, the property, the lives of individuals, is obvious to the narrowest and most unthinking minds. But, on the contrary, none but attentive and clear-sighted men perceive the perils with which equality threatens us, and they commonly avoid pointing them out. They know that the calamities they apprehend are remote, and flatter themselves that they will only fall upon future generations, for which the present generation takes but little thought. The evils which freedom sometimes brings with it are immediate; they are apparent to all, and all are more or less affected by them. The evils which extreme equality may produce are slowly disclosed; they creep gradually into the social frame; they are only seen at intervals, and at the moment at which they become most violent, habit already causes them to be no longer felt.

The advantages which freedom brings are shown by length of time; and it is always easy to mistake the cause in which they originate. The advantages of equality are instantaneous, and they may constantly be traced from their source.

Political liberty bestows exalted pleasures, from time to time, upon a certain number of citizens. Equality every day confers a number of small enjoyments on every man. The charms of equality are every instant felt, and are within the reach of all: the noblest hearts are not insensible to them, and the most vulgar souls exult in them. The passion which equality engenders must therefore be at once strong and general. Men cannot enjoy political liberty unpurchased by some sacrifices, and they never obtain it without great exertions. But the pleasures of equality are self-proffered: each of the petty incidents of life seems to occasion them, and in order to taste them nothing is required but to live.

Democratic nations are at all times fond of equality, but there are certain epochs at which the passion they entertain for it swells to the height of fury. This occurs at the moment when the old social system, long menaced, completes its own destruction after a last intestine struggle, and when the barriers of rank are at length thrown down. At such times men pounce upon equality as their booty, and they cling to it as to some precious treasure which they fear to lose. The passion for equality penetrates on every side into men's hearts, expands there, and fills them entirely. Tell them not that by this blind surrender of themselves to an exclusive passion, they risk their dearest interests: they are deaf. Show them not freedom escaping from their grasp, while they are looking another way: they are blind—or rather, they can discern but one sole object to be desired in the universe.

* * *

The American System

Henry Clay (1777-1852) first used the term "the American System" in a speech in Congress in 1824 defending the tariff. Clay's American System was a program for economic cooperation between the North and the West. Clay wanted high tariffs to be placed on foreign goods to protect the manufacturers of the North. Northern industrial products would then be traded for western agricultural products. The money from the tariff could be used for internal improvements, such as systems of transportation, which would benefit all sections of the country.

Southerners opposed the high tariff because it would interfere with their trade with Europe and raise the price of goods they needed. In February 1832 Clay delivered an address on the American System further defining his position. An excerpt from this address follows.*

---

*REGISTER OF DEBATES IN CONGRESS, 22nd Congress, 1st Session, VIII (Part I), 263 ff.

...The question, therefore, which we are now called upon to determine, is not whether we shall establish a new and doubtful system of policy, just proposed, and for the first time presented to our consideration; but whether we shall break down and destroy a long established system, patiently and carefully built up and sanctioned, during a series of years, again and again, by the nation and its highest and most revered authorities. And are we not bound deliberately to consider whether we can proceed to this work of destruction without a violation of the public faith? The people of the United States have justly supposed that the policy of protecting their industry against foreign legislation and foreign industry, was fully settled, not by a single act, but by repeated and deliberate acts of Government, performed at distant and frequent intervals. In full confidence that the policy was firmly and unchangeably fixed, thousands upon thousands have invested their capital, purchased a vast amount of real and other estate, made permanent establishments, and accommodated their industry. Can we expose to utter and irretrievable ruin this countless multitude, without justly incurring the reproach of violating the national faith? ...

When gentlemen have succeeded in their design of an immediate or gradual destruction of the American System, what is their substitute? Free trade! Free trade! The call for free trade is as unavailing as the cry of a spoiled child, in its nurse's arms, for the moon or the stars that glitter in the firmament of heaven. It never has existed, it never will exist. Trade implies, at least two parties. To be free, it should be fair, equal and reciprocal. But if we throw our ports wide open to the admission of foreign productions, free of all duty, what ports of any other foreign nation shall we find open to the free admission of our surplus produce? We may break down all barriers to free trade on our part, but the work will not be complete until foreign powers shall have removed theirs. There would be freedom on one side, and restrictions, prohibitions and exclusions on the other....

* * *

This brings me to consider what I apprehend to have been the most efficient of all the causes in the reduction of the prices of manufactured articles; and that is, *competition*. By competition, the total amount of the supply is increased, and by increase of the supply, a competition in the sale ensues, and this enables the consumer to buy at lower rates. Of all human powers operating on the affairs of mankind, none is greater than that of competition. It is action and reaction. It operates between individuals in the same nation, and between different nations. It resembles the meeting of the mountain torrent, grooving by its precipitous motion, its own channel, and ocean's tide. Unopposed, it sweeps everything before it; but, counterpoised, the waters become calm, safe and regular. It is like the segments of a circle or an arch; taken separately, each is nothing; but in their combination they produce efficiency, symmetry, and perfection. By the American System this vast power has been excited in America, and brought into being to act in co-operation or collision with European industry. Europe acts within itself, and with America; and America acts within itself, and with Europe. The consequence is, the reduction of prices in both hemispheres. Nor is it fair to argue from the reduction of prices in Europe, to her own presumed skill and labor . . . if our industry, by diminishing the demand for her supplies, should produce a diminution in the price of those supplies, it would be very unfair to ascribe that reduction to her ingenuity instead of placing it to the credit of our own skill. . . .

The great law of *price* is determined by supply and demand. Whatever affects either, affects the price. If the supply is increased, the demand remaining the same, the price declines; if the demand is increased, the supply remaining the same, the price advances; if both supply and demand are undiminished, the price is stationary, and the price is influenced exactly in proportion to the degree of disturbance to the demand or supply. It is therefore a great error to suppose that an existing or new duty *necessarily* becomes a component element to its exact amount of price. If the proportion of demand and supply are varied by the duty, either in augmenting the supply, or diminishing the demand, or vice versa, price is affected to the extent of that variation. But the duty never becomes an integral part of the price, except in the instances where the demand and the supply remain after the duty is imposed, precisely what they were before, or the demand is increased, and the supply remains stationary. . . .

But, it is argued that if, by the skill, experience, and perfection which we have acquired in certain branches of manufacture, they can be made as cheap as similar articles abroad, and enter fairly into competition with them, why not repeal the duties as to those articles? And why should we? Assuming the truth of the supposition the foreign article would not be introduced in the regular course of trade, but would remain excluded by the possession of the home market, which the domestic article had obtained. The repeal, therefore, would have no legitimate effect. . . .

. . . under the operation of the American System,

the products of our agriculture command a higher price than they would do without it, by the creation of a home market; and by the augmentation of wealth produced by manufacturing industry, which enlarges our powers of consumption, both of domestic and foreign articles. The importance of the home market is among the established maxims which are universally recognized by all writers and all men. However some may differ as to the relative advantages of the foreign and the home market, none deny to the latter great value and high consideration. It is nearer to us, beyond the control of foreign legislation, and undisturbed by those vicissitudes to which all international intercourse is more or less exposed. The most stupid are sensible of the benefit of a residence in the vicinity of a large manufactory, or of a market town, of a good road, or of a navigable stream, which connects their farms with some great capital. . . .

But if all this reasoning were totally fallacious—if the price of manufactured articles were really higher, under the American system, than without it, I should still argue that high or low prices were themselves relative—relative to the ability to pay them. It is in vain to tempt, to tantalize us with the lower prices of European fabrics than our own, if we have nothing wherewith to purchase them. If, by the home exchanges, we can be supplied with necessary, even if they are dearer and worse, articles of American production than the foreign, it is better than not to be supplied at all. And how would the large portion of our country which I have described be supplied, but for the home exchanges? A poor people, destitute of wealth or of exchangeable commodities, has nothing to purchase foreign fabrics. . . . The gentleman from South Carolina has drawn a lively and flattering picture of our coasts, bays, rivers, and harbors; and he argues that these proclaimed the design of Providence, that we should be a commercial people. I agree with him. We differ only as to the means. He would cherish the foreign, and neglect the internal trade. I would foster both. What is navigation without ships, or ships without cargoes? By penetrating the bosoms of our mountains, and extracting from them their precious treasures; by cultivating the earth, and *securing* a home market for its rich and abundant products; by employing the water power with which we are blessed; by stimulating and protecting our native industry, in all its forms; we shall but nourish and promote the prosperity of commerce, foreign and domestic.

I have hitherto considered the question in reference only to a state of peace; but a season of war ought not to be entirely overlooked. We have enjoyed near twenty years of peace; but who can tell when the storm of war shall again break forth? Have we forgotten so soon, the privations to which not merely our brave soldiers and our gallant tars were subjected, but the whole community, during the last war, for the want of absolute necessaries? To what an enormous price they rose! And how inadequate the supply was, at any price? The statesman who justly elevates his views, will look behind, as well as forward, and at the existing state of things; and he will graduate the policy which he recommends, to all the probable exigencies which may arise in the republic. Taking this comprehensive range, it would be easy to show that the higher prices of peace, if prices were higher in peace, were more than compensated by the lower prices of war. . . .

And now, sir, I would address a few words to the friends of the American System in the Senate. The revenue must, ought to be reduced. The country will not, after, by the payment of the public debt, ten or twelve millions of dollars become unnecessary, bear such an annual surplus. Its distribution would form a subject of perpetual contention. Some of the opponents of the system understand the stratagem by which to attack it, and are shaping their course accordingly. It is to crush the system by the accumulation of revenue, and by the effort to persuade the people that they are unnecessarily taxed, while those would really tax them who would break up the native sources of supply, and render them dependent upon the foreign. But the revenue ought to be reduced, so as to accommodate it to the fact of the payment of the public debt. And the alternative is, or may be, to preserve the protecting system, and repeal the duties on the unprotected articles, or to *preserve* the duties on *unprotected* articles, and endanger, if not destroy, the system. Let us then adopt the measure before us, which will benefit all classes: the farmer, the professional man, the merchant, the manufacturer, the mechanic, and the cotton planter more than all. A few months ago, there was no diversity of opinion as to the expediency of this measure. All, then, seemed to unite in the selection of these objects for a repeal of duties which were not produced within the country. Such a repeal did not touch our domestic industry, violated no principle, offended no prejudice.

Can we not all, whatever may be our favorite theories, cordially unite on this neutral ground? When that is occupied, let us look beyond it, and see if anything can be done in the field of protection, to modify, or improve it, or to satisfy those who are opposed to the system. Our southern brethren believe that it is injurious to them, and ask its repeal. We believe that its abandonment will be prejudicial to them, and ruinous to every other section of the Union. However strong their convictions may be, they are not stronger than ours. Between the points of the preservation of the system and its absolute repeal, there is no principle of union. If it can be shown to operate immoderately on any quarter; if the measure of protection to any article can be demonstrated to be undue and inordinate, it would be the duty of Congress to interpose and apply a remedy. And none will co-operate more heartily than I shall in the performance of that duty. It is quite probable that beneficial modifications of the system may be made without impairing its efficacy. But to make it fulfill the purposes of its institution, the measure of protection ought to be adequate. If it be not, all interests will be injuriously affected. The manufacturer, crippled in his exertions, will produce less perfect and dearer fabrics, and the consumer will feel the consequence. This is the spirit, and these are the principles only, on which, it seems to me, that a settlement of the great question can be made, satisfactorily to all parts of our Union.

Proclamation Against Nullification

In November 1832, a convention in South Carolina declared the tariff acts of 1828 and 1832 null and void. On December 10, 1832, President Jackson issued a proclamation which warned South Carolina that if it persisted with nullification it would act alone. With the subsequent lowering of the tariff, a crisis was avoided. This is a portion of Jackson's proclamation.*

Whereas, A convention assembled in the State of South Carolina have passed an ordinance by which they declare "that the several acts and parts of acts of the Congress of the United States purporting to be laws for the imposing of duties and imposts on the importation of foreign commodities . . . are unauthorized by the Constitution of the United States, and violate the true meaning and intent thereof, and are null and void and no law," nor binding on the citizens of that state or its officers. . . .

Whereas, By the said ordinance it is further ordained that in no case of law or equity decided in the courts of said state wherein shall be drawn in question the validity of the said ordinance, or of the acts of the legislature that may be passed to give it effect, or of the said laws of the United States, no appeal

*J. D. Richardson (ed.), MESSAGES AND PAPERS OF THE PRESIDENTS, Washington, D.C., 1898, Vol. II.

shall be allowed to the Supreme Court of the United States. . . .

Whereas, The said ordinance prescribes to the people of South Carolina a course of conduct in direct violation of their duty as citizens of the United States, contrary to the laws of their country, subversive of its Constitution, and having for its object the destruction of the Union. . . .

To preserve this bond of our political existence from destruction, to maintain inviolate this state of national honor and prosperity, and to justify the confidence my fellow-citizens have reposed in me, I, Andrew Jackson, President of the United States, have thought proper to issue this my proclamation. . . .

* * *

Look for a moment to the consequence. If South Carolina considers the revenue laws unconstitutional and has a right to prevent their execution in the port of Charleston, there would be a clear constitutional objection to their collection in every other port; and no revenue could be collected anywhere, for all imposts must be equal. It is no answer to repeat that an unconstitutional law is no law so long as the question of its legality is to be decided by the state itself, for every law operating injuriously upon any local interest will be perhaps thought, and certainly represented, as unconstitutional, and as has been shown, there is no appeal.

* * *

Under the Confederation then, no state could legally annul a decision of the Congress or refuse to submit to its execution; but no provision was made to enforce these decisions. Congress made requisitions, but they were not complied with. The government could not operate on individuals. They had no judiciary, no means of collecting revenue.

* * *

I consider then, the power to annul a law of the United States, assumed by one state, incompatible with the existence of the Union, contradicted expressly by the letter of the Constitution, unauthorized by its spirit, inconsistent with every principle on which it was founded, and destructive of the great object for which it was formed.

* * *

The Constitution of the United States, then, forms a government, not a league; and whether it be formed by compact between the states or in any other manner, its character is the same. It is a government in which all the people are represented, which operates directly on the people individually, not upon the states; they retained all the power they did not grant. But each state, having expressly parted with so many powers as to constitute, jointly with the other states, a single nation, cannot, from that period, possess any right to secede, because such secession does not break a league, but destroys the unity of a nation, and any injury to that unity is not only a breach which would result from the contravention of a compact, but it is an offense against the whole Union. To say that any state may at pleasure secede from the Union is to say that the United States are not a nation, because it would be a solecism to contend that any part of a nation might dissolve its connection with the other parts, to their injury or ruin, without committing any offense. . . .

* * *

Fellow-citizens of the United States, the threat of unhallowed disunion, the names of those once respected by whom it is uttered, the array of military force to support it, denote the approach of a crisis in our affairs on which the continuance of our unexampled prosperity, our political existence, and perhaps that of all free governments may depend. The conjuncture demanded a free, a full, and explicit enunciation, not only of my intentions, but of my principles of action; and as the claim was asserted of a right by a state to annul the laws of the Union, and even to secede from it at pleasure, a frank exposition of my opinions in relation to the origin and form of our government and the construction I give to the instrument by which it was created seemed to be proper.

Having the fullest confidence in the justness of the legal and constitutional opinion of my duties which has been expressed, I rely with equal confidence on your undivided support in my determination to execute the laws, to preserve the Union by all constitutional means, to arrest, if possible, by moderate and firm measures the necessity of a recourse to force; and if it be the will of Heaven that the recurrence of its primeval curse on man for the shedding of a brother's blood should fall upon our land, that it be not called down by any offensive act on the part of the United States.

Fellow-citizens, the momentous case is before you. On your undivided support of your government depends the decision of the great question it involves—whether your sacred Union will be preserved and the blessing it secures to us as one people shall be perpetuated. No one can doubt that the unanimity with which that decision will be expressed will be such as to inspire new confidence in republican institutions, and that the prudence, the wisdom, and the courage which it will bring to their defense will transmit them unimpaired and invigorated to our children.

May the Great Ruler of Nations grant that the signal blessings with which He has favored ours may not, by the madness of party or personal ambition, be disregarded and lost; and may His wise providence bring those who have produced this crisis to see the folly before they feel the misery of civil strife, and inspire a returning veneration for that Union which, if we may dare to penetrate His designs, He has chosen as the only means of attaining the high destinies to which we may reasonably aspire.